PELICAN

Girls and Sex

Wardell B. Pomeroy received his A.B. and M.A. in Psychology from Indiana University, and his Ph.D. from Columbia. As research associate at the Institute for Sex Research, he was co-author with Dr Kinsey of *Sexual Behaviour in the Human Male* and *Sexual Behaviour in the Human Female*. His *Boys and Sex* is a companion to this book and is a Pelican. Dr Pomeroy is also president-elect of the Society for Scientific Study of Sex, President of the American Association of Marriage Counselors, and a frequent contributor to professional journals. He is married, with three children.

D0587082

WARDELL B. POMEROY

Girls and Sex

PENGUIN BOOKS

Penguin Books Ltd, Harmondsworth, Middlesex, England
Penguin Books Australia Ltd, Ringwood, Victoria, Australia

—

First published by Delacorte Press 1969
Published in Pelican Books 1971

—

Copyright © Wardell B. Pomeroy 1969

—

Made and printed in Great Britain
by Hazell Watson & Viney Ltd,
Aylesbury, Bucks
Set in Linotype Pilgrim

This book is sold subject to the condition
that it shall not, by way of trade or otherwise,
be lent, re-sold, hired out, or otherwise circulated
without the publisher's prior consent in any form of
binding or cover other than that in which it is
published and without a similar condition
including this condition being imposed
on the subsequent purchaser

Contents

To my wife MARTHA,

whose loving and careful help

has made this a better book

Acknowledgements

THIS book is a natural sequel to the book *Boys and Sex*, published last year. It would not be possible to have written this book without the background of twenty years' experience at the Institute for Sex Research, Indiana University, Bloomington, Indiana, where I had the rare opportunity of interviewing 7,000 people about their sexual histories. Although a limited number were high school girls, a large number were former high school students and hence, at least in retrospect, were able to give me something of the flavour of their overt sexual behaviour and their dreams, their problems, their hopes and the outcomes of very diverse patterns of behaviour. As a refresher course, last Spring I met with several groups of high school girls in various parts of New York and New Jersey, to again remind me of what sex looked like from their vantage point. To those young ladies, ranging in age from thirteen to seventeen, I am very grateful.

I would like to express my very deep thanks to many of my friends who have taken time out from their busy schedules to read the manuscript and to make criticisms of it. Some of these criticisms were indeed extensive and many of them have been accepted, which, I am sure, has resulted in a better book. However, any errors are mine, not theirs. My particular thanks go to: Dr Mary Calderone, executive director of the Sex Education and Information Council of the United States, New York City; Dr Ruth Doorbar, psychotherapist, New York City; Dr Evelyn Gendel, physician, Topeka, Kansas; Dr Eleanor Hamilton, marriage counsellor,

New York City; Dr Warren Johnson, Department of Physical Education, University of Maryland; Dr Laurence H. Lang, II, Assistant Professor in Child Development, University of Connecticut, Storrs, Connecticut; Dr Eleanore Luckey, psychologist, University of Connecticut; Dr William H. Masters, Reproductive Biology Research Foundation, St Louis, Missouri; Dr Leah Schaefer, psychotherapist, New York City; Dr Laura Singer, marriage counsellor, New York City; Mrs Bunny Vincent, Supervisor of Research Interviewing, Bowman Gray School of Medicine, Winston-Salem, North Carolina; and Mrs Sally Williams, RN, Family Life and Sex Education, Anaheim, California.

As I mentioned in *Boys and Sex*, the book would never have been written without the encouragement and the writing talent of Mr John Tebbel. The same can be said for the present book. Working with Mr Tebbel is a freeing experience. I found that when I started to equivocate, he would say to me: 'Tell me what you want to say and I will see that it is said properly.' That is what has happened. Thanks.

Finally, I would like to thank my wife, Martha, to whom this book is dedicated. We read and re-read the original manuscript to each other, which proved very helpful in correcting errors of omission, of commission, and of emphasis.

W.P.

An Introduction
for Parents

PARENTS of teenage daughters today are more than usually troubled and confused about how much sex information to give them and what kind they should provide. They are even more concerned about trying to direct the overt sex behaviour of these daughters, who often seem grown-up too soon. Parents are embarrassed when talking about sex, as they have always been, and certainly the daughters don't give them much help, because they too are embarrassed and reluctant to discuss sex with parents. Most parents say nothing and keep their fingers crossed or else mutter vague warnings and occasionally issue stern prohibitions, which are often out of proportion to what the situation warrants.

It is my hope that parents will understand their own daughters better if they see them in relation to what is happening to young people and to sexual attitudes generally in Britain.

You, the troubled parent, read constantly about the 'sexual revolution' going on today, and you read about the hippies, free love, 'the pill' and its effects on the young, the radical change in the dress and appearance of both boys and girls, and the revolt of youth against the wisdom of its elders. Many of you are convinced that the world is going to the dogs generally, and you wonder where it will all end.

Things, however, are not so bad as they may seem. For

example, if one looks at the contemporary scene with a somewhat broader perspective, it is apparent that what we are witnessing is not a sexual 'revolution' but rather an evolution – changes occurring in a long, gradual development which is only one segment of a much larger change in social structures and institutions.

History offers a further consolation. A papyrus of 1700 BC is a lament by the elders in an Egyptian city about the young people of the community, who, in the language of our later day, also appear to be going to the dogs. The elders complain about the disregard of youth for authority. They are annoyed because the young boys are driving their chariots recklessly over the countryside without regard for life or limb. They are horrified that the young girls are shamelessly painting their lips with henna. Doesn't all that sound familiar?

It may not appear, in the light of the papyrus, that we have evolved much since the days of the Egyptians, but a steady process of evolution has, in fact, gone on. I believe the single most important factor in this process has been the changing role of the woman in our society, a change that was in turn caused by other social transformations, such as the one brought about by the industrial revolution, which in turn was precipitated by other alterations in the social structure, and so on backward through time.

Now that woman has emerged as a more equal partner with the male, we are witnessing a change in the double standard of sex morality and we have been confronted with the demand that the woman be accepted as the sexual being she is. But it must be remembered that the change in the role of women in our society is a long and continuing one, and so are the changes in sexual behaviour and attitudes.

One activity that seems to concern people of the older generation more than any other is premarital intercourse among young people. Those who are against it are simply opposed, and entertain no arguments about it. In reality, what we mean by saying that there is more premarital intercourse today is not at all clear. Do we mean an increase in incidence – that is, are more young people doing it? Is it an increase in frequency, meaning that young people are doing it more often? Is there any increase in the number of partners they are having – in other words, in promiscuity? Finally, is there a decrease in the quality of the relationship, call it 'love' or whatever you will, between young people engaging in premarital intercourse?

Few of those who deplore the 'sexual revolution' are able to supply answers to these questions. They are still more concerned about whether a girl stays a virgin until marriage, because the cult of the unbroken hymen is still with us.

We know that over the past forty to fifty years there has been a gradual increase in the amount of premarital intercourse, particularly at upper social levels, and no doubt there are continuing changes in the same direction. However, there is no evidence that the *rate* of increase has risen during this same period of time, which is one of the reasons I have come to conclude that our sexual mores are evolving rather than undergoing a revolution.

The social-class differences in sexual behaviour and attitudes which we recorded at the Institute for Sex Research in 1948 and 1953 still exist, but they are now diminished. At the lower social levels there is more acceptance of masturbation, nudity and variety in petting and coital techniques than in the past. At the upper levels, there is more acceptance of premarital intercourse.

Social change in sexual matters is evolving in other ways, too. One has only to look at the presentation of sex in literature, films, plays and other public media. It was in 1932 that an American newspaper, *The New York Daily News*, first carried the word 'syphilis' in print. Four years later Surgeon

General Thomas Parran first uttered the word on the radio. Another newspaper, *The New York Herald Tribune*, was first to use the word 'masturbation' – twenty years ago. Ten years ago there began to be sober discussions of homosexuality in the mass media, some of which were almost objective. Now it is difficult to find newspapers, books, magazines or plays which do *not* deal with all these subjects in one way or another, freely and openly.

Does this mean that there has been a corresponding change in overt sexual *behaviour*? Not necessarily, although a good many people think erroneously that one reflects the other. It does mean that there is a change in the open *discussion* of sex. Because of the increase in our population, there are more people and consequently more engaging in sexual behaviour of all sorts, thus presenting the misleading appearance of a higher rate of increase in sexual activity.

If I am correct in believing that our society is heading towards still more liberal attitudes to sex, the question arises as to what effect that will have. Those who view this trend with alarm predict it will lead to the decline and fall of our civilization, a moral bankruptcy comparable, as they are so fond of saying, to the collapse of the Greek and Roman civilizations. Yet I have never found a classical scholar willing to say that changing sexual habits had anything whatever to do with the fall of those civilizations.

On the other hand, there are the enthusiasts who go about proclaiming the advent of a splendid era of universal happiness and self-fulfilment. One gets the idea that the new sexual freedom will somehow decrease racial tension, obliterate war, improve the lot of the poor and lead us into more healthy, happy lives.

I think it is clear that both these groups are suffering from the same delusion. They believe mistakenly that sexuality is the primary moving force in human experience, and that its regulation or emancipation will somehow resolve all of mankind's problems. But sexual experience is more 'caused' than 'causing'. Sexual intercourse itself can be a deeply emotional and loving experience, as we all know, but it can also be an aggressive and hostile act, or no more than a casual toss on the mattress. The same thing can be said for any other kind of sexual behaviour.

The fact of the matter is that we really don't know as much as we think we do about sex. The amount of solid research data on sex behaviour is so meagre that we can truly say we are still in the Dark Ages. There are fewer than a hundred research projects in this field that could be said to meet the requirements of being statistically adequate, theoretically sound and pragmatically important. No other area of human behaviour remains so unexplored.

Nevertheless, our responsibility as parents for the sexual behaviour of our children does not diminish simply because we have inadequate knowledge at the moment. We must be guided by the information we have, and we must try to view our children's behaviour not in the light of our inherited prejudices but against the background of a changing world in which those children must grow up and become useful citizens.

It is particularly difficult to do this in the case of daughters. They occupy traditionally a protected position in society, and parents quite naturally find it a good deal easier to be objective about large questions like the changing role of sex in society than about the specific behaviour of their own daughters.

Parents have often asked me, 'How can I talk to my daughter about sex?' This question tends to come more often from mothers. Fathers are more likely to feel that it is not in their province, but something between mother and daughter. The question usually arises at about the same time as puberty, when parents observe secondary sex development in their daughter, or at the time when the daughter starts wanting to go out with boys. Very often these periods are closely related in time.

But to raise the question at that moment is to raise it about ten years too late. In the first place, I tell parents, you have been communicating with your daughter about sex from the time she was old enough to understand anything. *Not* talking with her about sex is communicating with her about it. In essence, not talking is telling your daughter that this is a taboo topic which is not to be discussed and must therefore be something special, secret, fearful and bad. Because you have instilled these feelings in your daughter by not talking to her about sex, she in turn will not broach the subject herself, nor will she come to you with her questions about it.

Parents have said to me many times, 'But my daughter is so young and innocent. She needs protection from all the ugliness and misery sex may produce in her later life.' But are they really protecting their children by trying to keep them in a state of ignorance? Isn't this ignorance at the root of so much sex-connected ugliness and misery? It is not so hard as it may seem to talk about sex with children. Every day there are opportunities for parents to bring up some aspect of the subject to a child of any age, without giving it undue emphasis.

What happens in school is a common enough topic of conversation at home. The talk often turns to feelings about a particular teacher, for instance. Frequently parents will tease a child about her feelings rather than discuss the fact that she is growing up and it can be expected that she may very well have these feelings about many people. Even an expression of dislike for a particular boy may be a cover-up for the beginnings of a sexual interest in him. All this, of course, needs to be expressed with some subtlety and without making the point too obvious.

Newspapers offer many opportunities. Parents and children often discuss the news casually, and teenagers many times ask questions about things they read in the paper. No newspaper is without stories involving sex, because it is so often news. Articles about contraception and population control, adultery, illegitimacy, child molesting, rape and other offences against the law provide opportunities to put into perspective what might otherwise be frightening or mystifying, and at the same time offer a chance to provide useful information about sex. Other stories of a less specifically sexual nature – censorship of books or films, war and its effects on people's sex lives – provide openings for discussion. Even a seemingly innocent subject like nutrition can be used to open up the subject of pubertal changes, since it is well established that good nutrition correlates highly with early puberty.

Whatever the discussion, parents should always remember the adolescent battle cry : 'Don't preach, don't lecture.' The discussion should be a calm, objective exchange of information and views, without making too much of a point of it.

Parents are often afraid to bring up sexual topics because they are afraid it will stimulate the child's interest in sex and that talking about it will lead to experimentation. They ignore the other side of the coin. Children who are baffled and unknowledgeable about sex will try to find out and this is more likely to lead to exploration and experimentation. In any case, children are going to explore their own bodies and those of their playmates, and even though it may sound like a frightening thing to some parents, I have seen no evidence to indicate that any harm is done by experimenting.

In other words, the issue is not what girls do sexually, but how they feel about what they do and what kinds of relationships they have with other people. These are the factors which will determine what sort of marriages they make and what kind of human beings they turn out to be.

Among the things I have tried to point out in this book are the differences between boys and girls which affect their attitudes and sexual behaviour with each other. One of the striking differences is that boys are more oriented towards their genitals and are much more concerned with genital activity, while the girl's sexuality is more diffuse and is much more concerned with the things surrounding sex than sex itself. The more boys and girls understand this, the better able they will be to understand the adjustments and compromises they will have to make in order to get along with each other.

Another difference is the greater concern the girl has for her reputation, not only where her peers are concerned but also with the adult world. Parents have helped to create this difference, and I'm afraid they will have to pay the price for it. The price is that girls are likely to determine what they do (and mostly what they don't do) on the basis of what other people may think about them, rather than on the basis of what their true feelings may be. Parents tell me they are teaching their daughters to be 'ladylike'. That means the social amenities – to be feminine, demure, non-aggressive, to keep their dresses down and their legs crossed, and not to chase the boys.

In the society we live in these are generally considered desirable attributes, but they are not attributes which lead towards a good sexual adjustment in marriage unless they are accompanied by teaching her to be a warm, open, responsive, sexually unafraid person. A young woman must unlearn her ladylike conduct in the bedroom and there revert to her more unrestrained nature in order to become a sexually responsive wife.

One of the ways this can be done is for the parents to be good models for their daughters. That means not only being willing to be openly affectionate towards their daughters, but also being that way with each other, so that the daughter can understand the meaning of a good, affectionate relationship between adults. With some parents, that might call for a revision of attitudes to the human body, because they must be willing to view it, male or female, with pleasure rather than with revulsion.

Finally, parents must be able to think in terms of their daughter's needs rather than of what the neighbours will think. In other words, they should be as open, relaxed and objective about sex as it is possible to be. To do that, it may be necessary for them to review their own sex lives and ask themselves, 'Has it been a life so perfect and satisfactory, so free of guilt and fear, that it has never given us any problems or affected the quality of our existence as individuals?' If the answer is no, the next question is unavoidable: 'Don't you want something better for your daughter?'

In this book, I have tried to provide the materials for the something that will be better, as far as a girl's sexual life is concerned. In the pages that follow, I have tried to supply the latest and most reliable information about the sex lives of girls in a way they will understand and that will help them to fulfil their roles in this complicated world.

1
A Girl's Sex Life

NOT long ago I wrote a book called *Boys and Sex*. It was written for boys themselves to read, rather than for their parents. I intended it for teenage boys, but as it turned out, some who were older and some younger ones read and appreciated what I had to say. This book is a companion volume, addressed directly to teenage girls rather than their parents. I suspect that a good many girls would find it equally informative to read the book for boys – and the other way around!

I have written *Girls and Sex* because I am convinced that, even though there is a great deal of talk these days about sex – in books, films, on television, and in conversation among and between boys and girls themselves – there is still nowhere girls can go to find answers to specific questions about sex and to hear a point of view that isn't moralistic or 'preachy'. Then, too, I had another reason for writing the book. I wanted to show girls what results might be expected from different kinds of sexual behaviour and the meaning that such behaviour could have for them.

'Meaning', of course, is not the same for everyone. Sex can mean many different things to different people. For some it means only reproduction. To others it means behaviour, like the changes in the body that occur when someone is sexually aroused. These changes can be the result of various kinds of psychological stimulation, or they can be the result of stimulation by the individual himself or by some other person.

Then there are people who have a much broader idea of

sex. To them it has to do, for instance, with how a girl acts and feels simply because she is a girl and with what her role as a girl is in our society. Many volumes could be written about this way of looking at sex, and many have been. I will have a few things to say about it in this book, but, in general, I am going to confine myself mostly to sex as a specific kind of behaviour and to talking about what meaning that behaviour might have for a teenage girl.

I am sure there are some parents and other adults who believe teenage girls are not ready for so much information about sex, and I suspect more of these people will be upset by *Girls and Sex* than by the book for boys. That is only natural. By tradition, girls are much more protected in our society. For my part, I believe sincerely that, if men and women are going to have sex relations with each other, both need an equal amount of information and it is unfair to put girls at a disadvantage by 'protecting' them.

Before they begin reading the information that follows, however, girls may rightly want to know what *my* attitudes to the subject are, where they are concerned. Let me say first that I think there is nothing wrong with the different attitudes boys and girls have to sex. It is not a question of which side is right. What we need is *understanding* of sex by both girls and boys, so that they can make an accommodation with each other and find fulfilment and happiness in each other.

I believe, further, that the question of whether a girl should engage in any kind of sexual behaviour depends on things like the attitudes of the people with whom she lives, especially those of her own age; the particular social level on which she lives; and whatever system of values, ethics or codes she has chosen to guide her, whether they are religious, or are something she has learned from her parents, or whether they rise from some deep inner conviction of her own. It is important, I think, that whatever a girl decides about sex, she should have as much information as possible on which to base her decision, and, of course, that is what I want to provide here. I intend to give girls as much information about sex in this book as I possibly can.

I have some other convictions about sex, too. I believe, for example, that there has been far too much emphasis on the question of intercourse before marriage. We have fussed and fumed and argued over it a long time now, and meanwhile it has become clearer than ever that what is far more important is the relationship between two people. How they feel about each other is what is important, not whether a penis enters a vagina.

My feeling is that sexual behaviour for both girls and boys is something both pleasurable and desirable as long as certain rules are followed. The rules are simple :

1. Nothing is done to hurt other people or to go against their wishes and desires – in brief, responsibility for others.

2. Whatever is done is not done so openly that it will get a boy or a girl into trouble with society.

On the other side of the coin, I would respect those who choose *not* to engage in any sexual experiences. That is their right.

These, then, are my attitudes, and I am sure every girl who reads these words has already begun agreeing or disagreeing with them. But what I hope is that my statements will impel her to examine more closely what her *own* attitudes are. Perhaps she isn't yet certain why she feels the way she does about sex, or she may not be exactly clear *how* she feels.

A good way to begin finding a path out of this confusion is to think for a minute about the real differences between boys and girls. It isn't just the obvious difference in anatomy. They are fundamentally different in their approach to life, in the roles they play in society and especially in their sexual lives. These differences are not always generally understood or appreciated by teenagers, and the misunderstanding accounts for much of the unhappiness they cause each other. Understanding sex is certainly not easy for adolescents, but, if it is any consolation, adults have a hard time, too. Sex difficulties are a factor, even though they may not be the chief one, in many divorces. Even for those who stay married, their sex problems may drive them to the doctor, the clergyman, marriage guidance or some other kind of therapy.

The basic problem is that boys and girls, and men and women as well, look at sex in different ways. It is not a question of who is right and who is wrong. The two sexes simply don't think about the subject in the same way. It is important for girls and boys to understand exactly what the differences are, because, if they do, they will have far more satisfactory sex lives as adults. If they understand, they will be able to make the necessary compromises and adjustments in their attitudes before they get into conflicts that may be hard to resolve. Obviously, the understanding has to be on both sides, so what I say now will be addressed to boys as well as girls.

To boys sex is often an awareness of changes in their bodies – physical changes that happen when they are sexually aroused. That may happen when they see pictures, read books, hear stories, think of sexy situations, if they touch persons of the opposite sex or even of the same sex, or if they touch their own bodies. Arousal means that the blood rushes to the surface of the skin and makes it warm, the penis hardens and becomes erect, increasing in size from about three and a half to six inches, the breath comes faster. These things can happen every day of their lives and usually do.

Girls are often unaware that this is what is happening to

boys, and don't know that it can even be a source of embarrassment to them, especially when they have to stand up in class and discover that they have an erection. Boys are upset to think that others will see the bulge in their trousers they can't conceal. When a boy is going out with a girl, sometimes the awkwardness and shyness he exhibits only means he is fighting against the sexual response he feels. Even though the girl is usually completely unaware of it, the boy would be deeply embarrassed if he thought she knew.

Girls, when they are aroused, go through the same kind of bodily changes boys do – that is, they feel warm and flushed and their breath comes faster. In place of the erection, they feel damp because of the lubrication of the vagina that has taken place. Girls of thirteen to seventeen who have not been aroused very much may be surprised if they find out that other girls have had such sensations.

In both boys and girls, if this kind of stimulation continues, it will increase in intensity until a pitch of excitement is reached which is nearly uncontrollable. Sometimes, at this point, there is a sudden release of sexual tension, followed by a quiet, relaxed, blissful feeling. This discharge of tension is what we call 'orgasm', or sexual climax. It occurs sometimes during petting, or during intercourse, or when a girl or a boy rubs his own sex organ, or it may happen at night while dreaming about sex.

Girls who understand why their response to sexual stimulation is not the same as it is for boys, even though physically the reaction may be so much the same, can see why it is that boys are able to feel more at home with sex. It is simply because it is so much part of their daily lives. For girls, in our society, it is a different matter. Times are changing, true, but most girls are still taught restraint where sex is concerned. In earlier days they were told constantly that they must always be 'ladylike'. The words may be different now but the intention is the same. Girls are not supposed to 'chase' boys. Parents make them come home at what the elders think is a reasonable hour, because a girl's reputation must be protected. Although these restrictions may irritate girls and cause friction at home, there is nothing particularly wrong with them except that, when a girl grows up and is ready to respond sexually, she may well discover that she has to unlearn her earlier behaviour if her sexual response is to be full and free. A wedding ceremony is no magic formula. It will not enable her to make the change suddenly.

It may take a girl weeks, months or even years after marriage to unlearn what she has been taught about being 'a lady'. In case anyone imagines it, I am not suggesting that a girl stop being a lady when she gets married. It is simply that, for a full and happy married life, she must learn to respond in the bedroom while she maintains a ladylike appearance the rest of the time. It is not always easy, but a great many brides learn how to do it, some of them quickly.

It is important for girls to understand this dual nature of their lives as soon as possible. They will not get much, if any, help from boys; few males understand that much about a girl's nature. They want a girl to be a lady, someone they can take out in public with pride, but at the same time nature has cast them in the role of the seducer, and without understanding what they are doing, they may try to convince the girl to be anything but ladylike. When they succeed, they are often shocked.

There are other fundamental differences between girls and boys. For example, by the time they are fifteen nearly all boys are having orgasm. They are having it, on the average, two or three times a week. For two thirds of them, their first orgasm came from masturbation; for one fifth from sexual dreams; and for less than one sixth, from petting. Less than one in ten had it from intercourse. Most

24

boys continue to have orgasm as a result of masturbation.

On the other hand, only about half of girls have been aroused at all by any means by the time they are fifteen. In the next five years, however, their lives change rapidly. By the time they are twenty, about nine out of ten have experienced some kind of arousal. Yet at fifteen, only a fourth of them have experienced orgasm from any source, and five years later, the figure is no more than half. About a third are aroused by masturbation, a third by petting, and another third, through psychological stimulation from books, pictures, fantasies, dreams or whatever. Two fifths of the girls experience their first orgasm from masturbation, one in twenty from dreams, a fourth from petting, one in ten from premarital intercourse, a surprising one in six from marital intercourse, and three per cent from homosexual contacts.

The boys who are having orgasm at fifteen, which includes nearly all of them, are having it two or three times a week, as I have said, and they are going out with girls of the same age, three fourths of whom are not having any orgasm at all and the other fourth only once every two weeks. No wonder there is trouble when people with such widely different sex experience first get together. It is easy to see why there is so much misunderstanding. The fact is that males are sexually mature and active at thirteen or earlier, while girls develop sexually much more slowly. A boy is at his sexual peak during adolescence and then becomes gradually less so as he grows older, although some men remain sexually active until they are in their nineties. Women, however, develop gradually until, at thirty, forty, or even fifty, they reach a peak of responsiveness almost as great as that of men. Consequently the troubles caused by the differences of adolescence go right on into adult life and are not easily solved unless there is real understanding on both sides.

This understanding, as I remarked a little earlier, is very much complicated by the roles in which society has cast boys and girls. Girls have the worst of it. They are not only different from boys, but there are important sexual differences among girls themselves, and somehow it seems hard for people to understand that there is a wide range of sexual interest and responsiveness among them. Boys, especially, usually have no idea that there are many girls who are simply uninterested in sex itself and who are not sexually aroused by pictures, books or by what they see in films. They are not, however, necessarily apathetic about boys. They may like boys and want to go out with them and enjoy their company, but sex has not yet become a part of their conscious lives.

At the other extreme are a small number of girls who are more easily aroused even than boys. They are aroused by seeing, reading and thinking of sexual things. They have orgasm frequently, quickly and easily, and often undergo a real struggle to keep out of trouble in a society which does not approve of such behaviour. They may also have difficulty in their own teenage society, if most of the other girls are not so uninhibited, which is usually the case.

Another large class of girls falls in the middle ground between these extremes, but it is a fact that most are far closer to the 'unresponsive' end of the scale than to the uninhibited end. This is particularly true of girls between the ages of thirteen and seventeen.

With all these differences among themselves, and between themselves and boys, girls often find it hard to adjust to the kind of society we live in, as I have noted. Society wants them to behave in a certain way and to live within certain rules laid down by the community in general; otherwise they will be looked down on. Society takes no notice of the wide range of differences among girls that

I have described above. It simply lumps them together as 'girls'.

If a girl gives in to a boy sexually, she is stepping out of her assigned role, and both she and the boy may wind up being extremely confused about what has happened to them. There is reason enough for confusion as it is. Girls grow up today in an atmosphere of freedom no other generation has ever enjoyed in this country. They are freer in every way but one – sexually. Society is softening in some respects about this, but, unless a girl rejects society completely, she may find that the penalties will be what they have always been if she steps out of her assigned role. It is no wonder that girls are so often confused by all the permissiveness they see and hear about, on one hand, and the social pressures that are put on them by parents and other members of the adult community on the other. Sometimes they don't know where to turn or how to behave.

Consequently, it may be fortunate that sex is not so much of a problem to girls as it is to boys, nor even so much as their parents may think it is. Sex is less important to girls than their public image or reputation. Boys, by contrast, are not so concerned about their sexual reputation; they may even be proud if it is an extensive one. But girls are painfully conscious of what other people think of them, and especially what other girls think. In spite of their freedom, they are fearful of getting a bad reputation, or of being known as an easy mark for boys who want sex, or of being outside the accepted social pattern.

Girls, in fact, seldom talk about sex as sex, and even when they do, they don't talk about it as boys do. Boys talk about sex a lot; they constantly trade information about it, even though much of what they think they know may be wrong. Girls' conversation, on the other hand, centres on dates and clothes and the personalities of individual boys, not on specific sexual activity. Their view of sex is essentially romantic, and that is something boys ought to know and remember.

When a girl is asked, 'Do you have any sex dreams at night?' she will often answer, 'Yes,' and if she is asked about the content of the dreams, the response will show quite clearly the difference between what girls and boys mean when they say 'sex'. The girl will say she has dreamed about walking down the aisle of the church at her wedding or being married and living in a house. If she says she has dreamed of making love with a boy, further questioning shows that what she means is not petting or intercourse, but some dreamlike, warm, affectionate relationship with a boy she likes.

This romantic, affectionate feeling is what a girl usually dreams about, awake as well as asleep, rather than some particular kind of sexual behaviour. Her night dreams and day-time fantasies are quite different from what boys are experiencing. A boy will dream or fantasize a specific, step-by-step description of a petting session with a girl, letting himself imagine in detail the experiencing of one sexual sensation after another. Girls are rarely so specific. For a girl, the fantasy, the dream is usually a full moon, a cool breeze, a warm and happy feeling of being with a boy she likes.

Girls might understand themselves better where sex is concerned if they could talk to their parents, but that is no more possible for them in most cases than it is for the boys. Few parents can talk to their daughters about sex, or vice versa. The embarrassment is likely to be even greater than with boys. Fathers, especially, find it difficult because they so often have such intense fears of their daughters' being involved sexually with boys. Partly that is because they are afraid a girl may get pregnant, but it is also partly due to their common reluctance to accept the fact that their daughters are maturing. In the normal course of events, fathers are jealous of this maturing and don't want to relinquish their daughters to boys, who are seen subconsciously as male rivals.

As for the mothers, they have lived through this adolescent period themselves and struggled with the same problems – how far to go with a boy, lack of real knowledge about sex, and all the other anxieties. And now they relive this period of uncertainty through their daughters. Naturally, they reflect and re-create whatever it was they experienced. Knowing these facts about parents won't necessarily solve the daughter-parent dilemma for most girls, but the knowledge may help them to understand what may often seem to them unreasonable attitudes on the part of their parents.

What other facts, then, should a girl know about sex as she grows up and lives through this difficult period of her life, after she has absorbed the fundamental differences between herself and boys?

I believe she ought to know something about the anatomy of the sexual parts of her own body and about that of boys. She needs to understand what causes the changes in her body when she is aroused sexually, as I described earlier. She ought to have some insight into her early sexual experiences and understand what effect they may have on her later life. It is also helpful to have more information about her social relations with boys, as in going out with them, and, even more specifically, about her sexual relations with boys, as in petting. I feel it will be helpful to her to know what intercourse is like and to understand the pros and cons of having it before marriage, especially in the ways it may affect her later life. I also think it is important for a girl to get more information about the stimulation of her own body and to have a better understanding of the meaning of sexual relations between members of the same sex. But especially she needs to know the difference between boys and girls when it comes to sexual behaviour and attitudes, in the ways I have described. It is this which will determine how well she is going to make a sexual adjustment in marriage.

Armed with all this knowledge, I am convinced that a girl will come to understand that she must be something of an actress in life. It will be clear that she has been given three roles to play. One is her role in society, first as a young girl growing up, then as a wife and mother, or as a career girl, or both, whatever the case may be. The second role is her relationship with boys, in which, as I have said, she must learn to be both ladylike and, eventually, unladylike when that kind of behaviour is required. The third role is perhaps the most difficult – the role she must play as herself, an individual responsible to herself.

No actress in the theatre could have a more difficult combination of roles. As an adolescent, a girl is engaged in learning how to adjust to society, to the adult world. Yet she must get along with boys, who have the same expectations of her as the adult world does and at the same time regard her as a sexual object. And in all of this, a girl has her own self, her own feelings, to consider. It is not easy.

I hope the information I have provided here and in subsequent chapters will truly help girls to play their triple role in a way that will bring them into the adult world with the best prospects for happiness.

2
The Body and Sex

IN this chapter we'll be talking about the various changes that develop in girls as they approach puberty and pass through it into adolescence – changes in body size and shape, in the breasts and in the sex organs. Along with these changes, I want also to talk about menstruation and about the way babies are conceived and born.

Usually, the changes begin about the time a girl is twelve years old. There is no hard and fast rule about this, however. Some girls have pubic hair and developing breasts when they are as young as eight or nine, while others do not exhibit these signs until they are fifteen or older. Why such wide variation exists is not too well known, but one of the major reasons is undoubtedly the inheritance a girl has from her parents, giving her a pre-disposition to develop late or early. Nutrition is another reason. Girls with better nutrition develop earlier, while those who do not eat properly as they grow up tend to develop later. People used to believe that girls who lived in hot climates developed earlier than those in the temperate zone, but this has been shown to be untrue.

Even though it makes no difference in a sexual sense whether a girl develops earlier or later, it does matter to her socially. Every girl gets some sense of well-being from the knowledge that she is like the people around her; consequently the early and late developers alike feel themselves different from their friends, like the very tall or the very short girl, and so they may be uncomfortable about it. It would be silly to pretend that these differences do not affect a girl's social outlook, but as far as sex development is concerned, there is certainly some consolation in the fact that, either way, the others will be like her eventually, or she will be like them.

Probably the part of their body development that girls worry about most is the breasts. They are soon aware that they will be more attractive to boys as they develop in that area, but they are often bothered and made unhappy by the emphasis which seems to be placed on these glands. Adolescent girls often worry a great deal, and quite needlessly, about their breasts. Mostly they are worried because they think them too small. A few are concerned about whether they are too large. There are a few other girls who worry that their breasts are developing unevenly. The fact of the matter is that breasts, like other parts of the anatomy, come in all sizes and seem to be attached to the body in a variety of ways. It is true that plastic surgeons can increase and decrease the size of breasts, but girls will later realize size is not so important as it seems to be in their teen years.

No doubt the trouble comes from the preoccupation with breasts we have experienced for the last twenty-five years or so. Girls with large breasts have been held up as objects of sexual admiration in advertising, in films and in a hundred other ways. All this makes girls with small breasts feel inferior and fearful that boys won't like them.

Nothing could be further from the truth. Few girls are built like Elizabeth Taylor or Gina Lollobrigida or Sophia Loren, yet they have no trouble finding boys to love them and marry them, even if they have small breasts. There are far more important things about a girl that interest boys than the size of these glands. It may console those with small breasts to know that breasts become larger during sexual arousal, sometimes by as much as twenty-five per cent. In any event, be sure that boys are going to like you for yourself, not because of the size of your brassiere.

Girls are often so preoccupied about the growth of their breasts, unfortunately, that they don't take the time to know and understand the rest of their anatomy. It is amazing how rarely girls ever examine their own sex organs, to see how they are put together. True, it is more difficult than for a boy, whose organ is visible and accessible. Usually a boy examines his own penis and scrotum; this is a universal characteristic of males. But if girls had a little more curiosity than most of them do, with the help of a hand mirror in one hand and parting their pubic hair with the other, they could understand their own anatomy considerably better.

What they would see, within the framework of the pubic hair, is that, first of all, they have one more body opening than the male. Both have, in common, the anus, through which the body's waste materials are excreted. There the resemblance ends. The boy has one other opening, at the end of the penis, through which he discharges his urine and the sperm-laden fluid of his ejaculation. The girl has a special opening to discharge urine and has a third opening, the vagina, between this and the anus. She also has, near the top of the vulva (which is the collective term doctors use for all those organs visible outside the body), the tiny penis-like organ called the 'clitoris'. This small organ has a rich supply of nerve endings and, when stimulated, provides sexual pleasure. The vulva is enclosed by two folds of skin – an outer one, the *labia majora*, and an inner one, the *labia minora*.

The vagina is a passageway between the external vulva and the internal sex organs, which include the uterus (or womb), the ovaries and the Fallopian tubes, all these encased within the protective framework of the pelvis, that part of the abdominal cavity which lies between the hip bones.

In every way, the vagina is a remarkable organ. Its walls possess an astonishing flexibility. A penis, no matter how large, will not test the capacity of the vagina, because its walls can stretch and stretch to permit the passage of a baby in birth – a truly remarkable thing when we remember that, on the average, the vagina is only three to three and a half inches long. It is an organ of many uses, designed to provide a canal for the menstrual flow, to receive the penis in intercourse, to hold the sperm cells when the male has discharged them and start them on their journey upward, and it provides the pathway for a baby's birth.

The vagina is lubricated a little by fluid from glands in the cervix, to which it is attached at the upper end, and a little more by other glands located near the outer opening. But mostly it is lubricated by internal secretions from its own walls – like sweat on the body – when these walls get warm in response to sexual stimulation. A girl will feel these secretions – 'feel wet' around the vulva and possibly on her thighs – when she is sexually aroused. Over the entrance to the vagina is a thin membrane called the 'hymen', with an opening in it. This opening allows the girl to menstruate and the hymen is pliable enough for a tampon to be inserted. During the first intercourse, the hymen is stretched or broken so that the penis may enter the vagina. When this happens, there is a slight bleeding and a quick pain which, in most cases, is soon over. Sometimes it is broken so easily a girl does not even know when it happens. At the other extreme, a membrane may be so tough that occasionally a doctor may be required to break it.

A girl is usually first conscious of her sex organs at adolescence when she begins to menstruate. That happens most often about a year after the appearance of pubic hair and the beginning of breast development. Again, however, there is variation among girls and it may not happen precisely at that time. There is no reason to worry if menstruation does not occur until later. As with other symptoms of sexual development, whether it is early or late has no particular meaning.

Some girls feel badly about the adolescent changes in their bodies because life becomes different from what they've been accustomed to for so long. Others don't like the idea of growing up. In either case, they're likely to think that menstruation is a messy business, and if they have cramps, aches and pains as well, they resent this intrusion on their well-being every month. When they realize that it is something that is going to happen to them for the next twenty-five to forty years, a few girls are seized with a kind of despair, feeling themselves trapped. Most girls, however, take a different view of it. They are pleased by the onset of menstruation because they *do* want to grow up, and they understand that this is one of the most important parts of that process. Menstruation means becoming a woman, and they are then capable of having children.

Menstruation can also take on a happier appearance when there is an understanding parent involved. I know one father who observed the occasion of his daughter's first menstruation by bringing her flowers and making a little ceremony of the fact that now she had become a young lady. That daughter could not help feeling proud and pleased about becoming adolescent.

Still, for many girls, menstruation comes as a dismaying shock. Since there is so little communication between parents and children about sex, these girls are unprepared for it. When it does begin, most mothers instruct their daughters what to do about it and inform them that it will be with them most of their lives. But they usually give the girls precious little information about what precisely is happening to them.

There is nothing at all mysterious about menstruation. What has happened inside the girl's body is that her ovaries have begun to function. These organs, one on each side of the uterus, carry the eggs which create another life when they are combined with a male sperm. In most instances, one of these eggs matures every month, and about half-way between periods of menstruation, it breaks loose from the follicle which encloses it in the ovary and moves down into the Fallopian tube. This follicle is only a covering for the egg, but it also has the function of producing the female sex hormone, oestrogen. This hormone provides a girl with the characteristics identifying her as female and the companion ovarian hormone, progesterone, also prepares the uterine lining for pregnancy, if the egg is fertilized by the sperm.

The follicle, after the egg has left it, changes colour and becomes something else, called 'the yellow body'. It is larger now and begins to affect the lining of the uterus, causing it to produce blood pools concentrated under the cell layers, so that the baby will have oxygen and food if conception occurs.

But if fertilization does not take place, the whole scene changes. The egg simply disintegrates in a few hours and is gone. The yellow body disappears, too, since it no longer has any purpose. What remains are the blood pools it created, but since the body is not equipped to take these back into the circulatory system, the blood and the cell layers in the lining of the uterus slip out through the vagina. That is what we call 'menstruation'. Girls who are afraid because they think they are passing so much blood should know that they are losing only about one to three ounces of it. Nor is this menstrual blood like the blood that spurts out when she cuts herself, because it is mixed with the mucous membrane from the womb. A girl should not feel squeamish about it, as some do. Actually, some people have intercourse during menstruation and feel entirely comfortable about it.

There is no reason to worry if menstruation is irregular when it first begins. Several months sometimes elapse between the first and second time, and irregularity is perfectly natural among young girls. It only means that the ovaries haven't begun producing mature eggs on a regular basis. No reason, either, to worry about the length of the period. Sometimes it takes only three days, sometimes as much as seven. Five days would be the average, but a girl might not always menstruate for the same number of days.

Another variation in the process is the way menstruation affects a girl mentally and physically. Some girls have their periods regularly, have no forewarning until it begins, and no symptoms of any kind, except perhaps a feeling of fullness. Others not only have a common symptom, cramps, but they feel depressed and vaguely unhappy; their bodies seem heavy and lumpy, and they are listless and tired for a day or two. A combination of psychological and physical factors, like congestion, may produce this feeling. Aspirin and a little mild exercise are the best remedies. The only danger is that a girl will take her symptoms so seriously that she will use menstruation as an excuse to retreat from life into illness every month, to gain attention or to avoid some real-life situation.

There is no need for a girl to feel crippled or 'out of the running' when she's menstruating. If she does, she should see her doctor. She can do nearly everything she is accustomed to doing, except that it is probably a good idea not to exercise too violently on the first day. But it is only a superstition that a girl can't take a bath or a shower or go swimming or wash her hair when she menstruates. The only thing she needs to be a little careful of is to avoid getting chilled, because her body is more susceptible to chilling at that particular time. A healthy girl can exercise, go to classes, work, go to parties or do anything else she likes while she menstruates. She'll feel better if she gets enough sleep and if she takes in more fluids than usual, like fruit juice and milk, and avoids rich, starchy foods. But, then, that's good advice in general.

One thing that bothers some girls is the odour of menstruation and the increased activity of the sweat glands. That is easily counterbalanced by paying attention to personal hygiene, using deodorants under the arms and on the sanitary pads. Pads or tampons should be changed frequently.

Some girls like pads, others prefer tampons. Many use pads the first day or two, then switch. The choice is personal. There may well be, in my opinion, a good psychological reason for using tampons, however, because they teach a girl what it is like to have something in her vagina and quite possibly will make her feel more comfortable when she finally has intercourse. Sometimes a girl needs to be taught how to insert them properly. They should not be forced in. Often it is helpful to lubricate the tip of the tampon before insertion. Even with minimal flow, they should be changed every eight hours. There is no truth, incidentally, in the old wives' tale that using tampons will cause cancer.

Menstruation is not the only kind of discharge to come from the vagina. Sometimes there will be a slight bloody staining between periods, but it is nothing to worry about; it may happen as the egg leaves the ovary and moves down into the uterus. A girl may even feel a little pain on one side or the other for a brief time. This is not true of all women, and those who experience it may have it for half an hour to a day. If, however, there is genuine bleeding between periods, much thicker and darker than the staining, or if her periods are very difficult, a girl should consult her doctor at once, because such bleeding is not normal and the difficulty may require medical attention.

Another kind of vaginal discharge which may occur is a seepage of fluid ranging in colour from white to yellow, and often with a noticeable odour and with some itching or burning. This is sometimes caused by a fungus growth resulting from germs which have found their way into the vagina. It should have the attention of a doctor, who can cure it easily with medication. Girls ought not to feel so embarrassed about it that they won't even tell their mothers. If they do nothing, the infection may continue for some time. They should remember that it is no more special than a minor infection anywhere else in the body. The best advice is, tell your mother and get it taken care of promptly by the doctor.

Now let's see what occurs when the vagina is penetrated by a male penis in intercourse and pregnancy results. Surprisingly, even in our era of freedom, this process is not really understood by many girls. Nor is it such a simple cause-and-effect relationship as it may seem. When the male ejaculates, he pours his semen into the vagina. This semen contains millions of sperm cells, whose long tails begin to lash, moving them forward until they enter the cervix, which is the passageway into the uterus, or womb. The uterus is pear-shaped, looking a little like the head of a very small bull. Its 'horns' are the Fallopian tubes, connecting the uterus with the ovaries. The sperm swim from the cervix into the uterus and up through these 'horns'. There they may or may not encounter an unfertilized egg cell coming down from an ovary on the once-a-month descent through the tubes.

If the sperm encounter an egg in the tubes, a bombardment of it results as the tiny sperm cells, lashing their tails, surround it and try to penetrate it. Pregnancy occurs when a sperm cell enters through the egg wall and merges with the egg, after which the cell wall immediately hardens up so that no more sperm can get in. The sperm cell that did the fertilizing becomes a part of the egg's nucleus. The other sperm die in a few hours. This whole process, from ejaculation to the encounter with the egg cell, may take as long as eight hours.

When sperm and egg join, fertilization takes place, and the baby is conceived at that moment. Sperm carrying Y chromosomes make boys; those with X chromosomes make girls. Sex is determined by whichever kind of sperm cell fertilizes the egg cell, and this is a matter of pure chance. Chance, in fact, is a large part of the whole process. The sperm must be in the Fallopian tubes at a time when the egg is travelling through it. It must be a vigorous sperm and the egg must be ripe. A woman produces only about 400 ripe eggs in her entire lifetime, and there are only about twelve to twenty-four hours in every month when it is possible for a ripe egg to be fertilized. If these odds against pregnancy encourage a girl and a boy to 'take a chance', they should remember that sexual Russian roulette is a dangerous game, and in the end, the odds are against them and the risk far too great.

Just as there are so many misconceptions about getting pregnant, there are probably nearly as many about childbirth. Girls sometimes hear so many horror stories about the agony of birth and the distress of pregnancy itself that they are badly frightened of getting pregnant even when they are married and, if they do, live in a state of fear until the baby comes.

They should know that the pain isn't all that bad by any means. Girls who start worrying about how something as large as a baby could come out of anything as small as a vagina should remember the incredible stretching capacity of that organ. It is the stretching that hurts, of course, but many women have learned to have little fear or pain by learning the techniques of natural childbirth. For those who find themselves unable to accept these techniques, modern anaesthetics can help to decrease the pain. In any case, there is little danger in properly supervised childbirth these days. For one thing, women see their doctor regularly during their pregnancy, and he is consequently able to anticipate any possible complication. While it is true that complications may occur, the chances of their happening are extremely low. As for the complications which may occur during the last three months, the odds are about one in 200, and even then doctor and patient, working together, can either prevent any trouble or take care of it properly as soon as it happens.

Whatever discomfort is involved during pregnancy or birth is more than made up for, as millions of women will testify, by the special joy of giving birth to a baby, an experience women alone can know.

This, then, is the cycle of change in a girl from the time of her beginning adolescence until she has her first child. The girls who read this book will be in the first part of the cycle, I assume, and I hope that I've given them here the information they need to understand how their bodies are constructed, and encouraged them to investigate and appreciate how really marvellously equipped they are to function as one half of the male-female relationship. I hope, too, that I've reassured them about what is happening to them and what will happen.

The culmination of physical development in a girl comes usually at about the time she reaches sixteen. For girls who are sixteen and have still not reached that point let me add that there is a wide variation. Some girls reach their full development as far as growth and height are concerned by the time they are ten or eleven years old. Others do not achieve it until they are twenty-one or older. And even when growth and height are complete, there is still further development in the breasts and the growth of pubic hair, while the girl's figure may keep on filling out for some time until it has reached the proportions she will have as a woman.

Thus, becoming adolescent can be a joyous and happy time, yet it *is* a time of change and adjustment. For some that means anxiety and fear, but I believe a girl who possesses the knowledge of her body detailed in these pages will find some help in enjoying the process of growing up that every girl must go through.

3

Early Sexual Experiences

BOYS and girls are often curious about what the sex organs of the opposite sex look like. By the time they are five years old, a fair number of girls have seen a boy's penis. Often their first sight of it is a younger brother's, while he is being changed or bathed as his sister watches. However, a few girls of thirteen still have never seen the penis on a living male. Even if they have a baby brother, their parents mistakenly keep them carefully protected from viewing it. Naturally, such overprotection on the part of the parents only serves to whet the desire of the girl to see something that is forbidden. Worse, it may make her fearful and ashamed of looking at it, which can only cause trouble later on.

This hiding away of the penis is one of the more foolish things parents do about sex. Not only can it result in psychological damage, but any girl who reads magazines or books or takes art classes in school soon sees the penis reproduced in works of art, both paintings and sculpture. The great masters have reproduced it endlessly through the ages, just as they have similarly depicted the entire male body in all its splendour. Museums are filled with their testimonials to the beauty of the human form, both male and female. If a young girl has been given the idea that the penis (and the nude male body) is ugly or repulsive, she will have a great deal to overcome when she is older and trying to enjoy sex with her husband.

The girl who sees her little brother's or some other boy's penis in the casual pattern of everyday living learns to accept this male equipment as a fact of life. If it is hidden away from her, she will keep on wondering about it, and the secrecy may contribute substantially to any troubles which may arise in her own life later.

Before girls become adolescent about half of them have seen their father's penis or that of an older male relative. It is little different to them than seeing a baby's or a small boy's penis. These are simply things males have, and their curiosity is at least partially satisfied about males. Seeing the male sexual organ and having sexual contact with adult males are two different things, however, and I will discuss that problem later on in this chapter.

It has always been a natural part of a child's development to look at and explore the bodies of other young children, to examine the similarities and differences, and to get some sexual pleasure from doing it. Mistakenly again, parents forbid this harmless sexual activity. It's naughty, they say, and so they should not be surprised that children try even harder to do this naughty thing their parents are forbidding and find extra spice in doing it because of the parental attitude. The children go right on playing the ancient games of childhood – mummies and daddies, doctor and nurse, and all the others the parents played, too, but which some of them seem to have forgotten. Young children use these games as a way to look at and explore each other's bodies.

Once children learn that these activities are considered 'naughty' – and sometimes they learn this from other children – they rarely tell their parents they're doing it. Consequently, when many parents accidentally discover that their children are having sex play, they become terribly upset and blow up the incident out of all proportion to its real significance. Often, with such a scene, the gap between the generations first begins to open, and it will not be long, if the attitudes persist, before parents find themselves absolutely unable to talk openly to their children about sex. The children, for their part, continue to carry on their sex lives and normal sexual development secretly.

There is nothing in the least unusual or 'dangerous' about this early sex play. About half the time it consists of nothing more than looking at the organs of the opposite sex. A girl may touch the boy's penis, and the boy will touch her vulva. It is a process of exploring with the hands rather than with the eyes. Occasionally very young boys and girls may try having intercourse with each other. In most of these cases there is no actual penetration by the penis. It is more a matter of the boy getting on top of the girl and going through the motions. Rarely at this age would they understand what actually happens in intercourse. A few (but very few) others try to insert something into the girl's vagina – a finger or a stick – and even fewer have the idea of trying to put their mouth on the other's sex organ.

For nearly all girls, such early play is done without any sexual arousal on their part. Perhaps only one out of ten gets a feeling she can identify later as an arousal. For the few girls who are aroused, however, the experience can lead to orgasm (see Chapter 6), one as full and complete and satisfying as those they will have when they are older. Even baby girls, less than a year old, are quite capable of having these orgasms, and sometimes they do.

In general, girls tend to have more sex play at younger ages, from four to nine years of age, than they do at older ages, from ten to thirteen. For half of the girls who experience early sex play, it is something that happens only once, or two or three times at the most. For the others, it will happen oftener and the experiences may be spread out over the entire pre-adolescent period.

Girls also sometimes have sex play with other girls. This happens about as often as sex play with boys. It, too, is usually just exploration and curiosity rather than deliberate attempts at sexual arousal. About a third of the time, such play is concerned only with looking, while the other two-thirds go so far as to touch. In two out of ten cases, it will involve inserting fingers or other objects into the vagina – and, incidentally, this happens much more frequently between girls than between boys and girls. Rarely, as in sex play with boys, do these experiences between girls involve what we call 'oral-genital contact' – that is, the mouth on the sex organ.

By and large, boys are more inclined to have sex play before adolescence than girls are. Not infrequently one girl may be involved in sex play with two or more boys at the same time, but less frequently is a single boy involved with two or more girls simultaneously. Boys are also more likely to start sex play with girls than the other way around.

Sex play with boys (or, for that matter, with girls) can be exciting, pleasurable and even worthwhile in the sense that it will help later sexual adjustment. But there are three difficulties which make the whole thing complicated. One is the possibility of being found out by parents or other adults and so having the experience exaggerated beyond its simple significance, as I pointed out earlier. A child is likely to be punished for it or made to feel unworthy or wicked in some other way, because most adults are convinced such behaviour is wrong and dangerous.

The second difficulty is somewhat like the first. Other children involved in sex play often reflect attitudes about sex, even though they may be taking part in the play themselves. If they know someone else has been caught doing it, they may ridicule the girl who has been found out, or her playmates may shut her out of their circle. The third problem is the feeling of guilt that some girls develop whether they are caught or not. The realization that this play must be kept secret and that it is disapproved of develops feelings of being naughty and of being not worthwhile.

I presume the girls who are reading this book have already lived through that part of their lives, and so whatever they did one way or the other is now past. But I hope that those who did engage in sex play as children will be able to see now that there were positive and worthwhile aspects about it, no matter what negative things may have bothered them. They may be able now to put those 'bad' things in a little better perspective.

In the first chapter I mentioned that boys are much more interested in sex in a specific way than girls are. It isn't surprising, then, that older men get interested in young girls and hope for some sort of sexual response from them. At least a quarter of the girls who reach adolescence have been approached by older men, or perhaps have even had direct sexual contact with them. By the time they are seventeen, nearly all girls have had such approaches made to them, in one way or another.

These approaches are often harmless, like the appreciative whistles from strangers in the street or from passing lorry drivers. They range from whistles to what may be a half-joking sexual advance from a girl friend's father, who puts his arm around her from behind and presses on her breasts, or strokes her buttocks affectionately, or likes to put his arms around her. Again, it may be the loving uncle who enjoys patting his niece's thigh or some other part of her anatomy. Even more frequently, perhaps, it may be a direct sexual advance from a young father who is taking the baby-sitter home. Approaches can be merely verbal, or they can go as far as exposing the penis or touching a girl's sex organ or, if a man gets the response he hopes for, actual intercourse.

Girls are often embarrassed and bewildered about how

to handle these situations. They often feel threatened by them and uncomfortable. The approaches are usually uninvited and unexpected, but sometimes girls, whether they realize it or not, encourage a man to make an advance.

Let me talk first about the ones that are uninvited. When she is being approached by an older man and hasn't invited it, one of the things a girl can do is to let him know flatly and at once that she isn't interested. No need to be hysterical about it – just firm. If the girl is confused and taken aback by the advance, she may well be hesitant and silent, not knowing what to say or do, utterly embarrassed by the whole thing and unable to handle the situation. Unfortunately, a man is likely to take her silence for consent, even though she is far from consenting. A complicating factor is that such a young girl feels herself in the presence of a more powerful person, an authority figure like her parents, and believes she cannot deal with him as she would a boy of her own age.

She ought to remember that it is a situation where she has every right to let her feelings be known, and afterwards, aware of what has happened, she will be much more careful not to let herself be put in such a position again. Sometimes, though, it can't be anticipated – as in the case of the girl friend's father, or the father of the baby she has been sitting with. In these situations, a good idea is to think of it as no different than being out with a boy one doesn't like well enough to pet with. The tentative advances he makes are about the same thing, and it is entirely proper for her not to be awed by his greater age and authority.

There are many situations, however, where a girl consciously or unconsciously invites approaches from older men. Sometimes the sheer pleasure of knowing that an older man is attracted to her, or has singled her out to pay attention, makes her act in a flirtatious or seductive manner. Then things may get out of hand because the man becomes more aggressive than the girl likes or knows how to handle.

Sometimes men (mostly strangers) expose their penises to a young girl because of mental problems which drive them to it. They may do this in the mistaken hope a young girl will become interested. More often, however, they do it to provoke a reaction of shock, revulsion or surprise which may follow the exposure. Men who do this are almost never dangerous, and the best possible way to deal with them is to show complete indifference and keep cool. Confronted with such a situation, the girl may think that it is the exhibited penis which is ugly and repulsive. In reality, it is the circumstances surrounding the act which are repellent, not the penis itself.

Another not uncommon experience occurs when a girl goes alone to the cinema and a man sitting beside her slips a hand under her thigh or otherwise makes some kind of sexual advance. The remedy is a simple one. Get up and move to another seat. If he persists, call the usherette.

Society, as I have noted, frowns on sex play between children. However, it must be remembered that society disapproves of a great many sexual acts that take place, and, as with most other things, there are two sides to the story. Granted, there are sometimes good reasons for the disapproval, but on the other hand, there is also a large amount of over-reaction to sex on society's part. If a girl has had sex play with girls and boys of her own age, I hope these experiences have been or will be of value to her, whether they turned out well or badly. If badly, she may have learned as she would from any other unhappy and upsetting experience. If well, she has learned something positive – about the way her own body works and what its reactions can be, and something about other people, too. Pleasure has been given and received. All of these things have their values for the future.

4
Going out with Boys

GOING out with boys ought to be an easy and pleasant matter, a learning process that paves the way to adult relationships, both sexual and nonsexual. Often it is, but as a matter of common observation, there are few areas of boy-girl relationships where more problems arise. Parents know it, teachers know it, every writer of an advice column knows it, and most of all, painfully and with some heartache, girls and boys know it. Too often, adults smile and dismiss this adolescent struggle as part of the business of growing up, and, of course, it is. That implies, however, that there is nothing to be done about it and consequently nothing to be disturbed about. But better understanding can improve any kind of human relationship, and adolescent relationships are no exception.

One of the first things to understand is the marked difference in the way girls and boys grow up at this stage of their lives. It accounts for a good part of the trouble. The fact is that, on the whole, girls grow up faster than boys. Their height starts increasing rapidly a year or more before the boys begin to shoot up, and for thirteen- and fourteen-year-olds, this difference creates a potentially embarrassing situation. A girl finds that she has suddenly begun to look over the head of the boy she has liked and played with since they were children, and it may be two or three years before they are back on even terms. Meanwhile, social customs being what they are, girls may not want to go out with boys who are shorter, and quite naturally many boys, who are just beginning to go out with girls about this time, find such discrimination hard to understand. As a consequence, younger girls who haven't begun to grow that much may find themselves seeing boys a little older than they are. Still other girls are late starters or naturally shorter, so there is some evening up of opportunities.

Girls also mature earlier than boys. The pubic hair around the girl's sex organ usually grows before the male's, and her breasts enlarge before the corresponding breast knots on the boy begin to swell. On the average, she menstruates about a year before the boy is able to ejaculate. There is a reverse difference here, however. The boy has sperm in his semen from the first, while it is probably true, although not absolutely proven, that a girl does not produce egg cells that are capable of fertilization at the time of her first menstruation. It may take her several months or even years before this process, called 'ovulation', begins. We know, however, that this is not true of all girls.

As I have pointed out earlier, an important difference at this stage is the fact that most boys suddenly become intensely interested in sex, while most girls do not. Girls *are* interested in boys in a way they haven't been before, true enough, but they think of their new relationship in terms of going out and having a good time, while the boy is sexually excited and feels an urge, perhaps unconsciously, towards ejaculation. Girls seldom know how boys are feeling at this particular time, and most of them are astonished if they find out they have excited a boy sexually by flirting or petting. As far as the girl is concerned, it's only another kind of friendship.

In spite of these difficulties, going out is something both sexes want very much to do. This urge raises the question that bothers so many girls, and boys, too: 'How do I find someone to go out with?' So many are eager to start, but don't know quite how to begin.

A girl can look at the problem in familiar terms. It's like going to buy a dress. If a girl wants new clothes, she has to go to a store that sells dresses – and that's the way it is where boys are concerned. The easiest place to look, of course, is in school, where girls are in daily contact with boys their own age; most pairing up begins right there. Students in girls' schools have a little more difficult time, but even there, school authorities frequently arrange parties and other events to bring boys and girls together. There are other places, too. Young people's groups in churches are good places to meet boys, and community clubs are often available. Sometimes parents can be persuaded to take the kind of summer holiday that would put a girl in a situation where she would meet boys. Summer jobs, either at resorts or in the city, provide further opportunities. Still another approach is to choose girl-friends who are already going out with boys; that often leads to meeting friends of their friends.

Meeting boys is sometimes easy, sometimes difficult, but in either case, it is only the beginning. Many girls try all the approaches I have listed and still they don't have boy-friends. Why? Most commonly, it is because of a girl's attitude towards herself. I tell such girls: 'It's difficult for other people, including boys, to like you unless you like yourself.' At first, they don't understand what I mean, because it is common belief that people grow to like themselves as other people demonstrate a liking for them. However, self-approval is a highly important element in living happily, and it comes from the individual's view of himself.

What does it really mean to 'like yourself'? For one thing, it means a girl isn't obsessed with her physical imperfections. She is not absorbed in the knowledge that her teeth are slightly crooked, or that she has a great many freckles, or her hair is not the colour she'd like to have it, or her figure isn't as good as her friend's. Physical qualities are far from being the whole sum of beauty. Some of the most beautiful girls I've known would never be able to get into a beauty contest. And conversely, some beauty contest winners have been the worst possible candidates for establishing a good relationship with a boy. Girls who think that boys like only the prettiest girls are looking at the wrong boys. Those who are hung up on how beautiful a girl is are not good candidates for boy-friends, in any case.

Many aspects of a girl's relationship with herself can get in the way of successful dating. There are girls who have personality problems of different kinds, like those who are in such extreme (not the usual) rebellion against their parents, that this situation becomes very nearly the most important thing in their lives. Others are in constant conflict with their brothers and sisters, and that absorbs their emotions. Others have strong guilt feelings about things they may have done, and can't lift their eyes above the high wall these feelings have erected between them and the world. Then there are the lonely girls, usually painfully shy. All these types have the poorest prospects for going out with boys.

The obstacle such personality difficulties raise is that a girl becomes so concerned with herself and her problems that she is unable to see a boy as an individual in his own right, a human being with his own feelings and desires. That's what I mean when I tell girls they have to like themselves before other people will like them. It doesn't mean being egotistical. It means they must believe they're as good as anyone else.

By this time the girls reading this book may be muttering, 'That's a lot of preaching. How do I start liking myself?' I have to confess that there is no easy answer to this question, and I would not pretend there is. But I am certain any girl can make a start simply by recognizing that she is going to be much happier if she understands something has to be done and begins to make an inventory of her personality to see where she needs to change.

I remember a girl who had already won a beauty contest and who came to me with a surprising complaint. She was convinced that she was really ugly and that boys were interested in her only because of possible sex and didn't think of her as a person. I saw how useless it was to try to reassure her about her beauty; she would only think there was something wrong with me because I couldn't see, or wouldn't admit, her ugliness. As we began to explore why she thought she was ugly, I discovered that she was carrying many guilt feelings about sex play she had enjoyed when she was very young. When these were resolved in her mind, she was able to accept herself as she actually was and learned that boys could relate to her as a person, not merely as a sexual object.

Another patient I recall is a girl who came to me because she was preoccupied with a feeling of being rejected by her father, which was, in fact, the case. She had to learn to accept the truth that simply because her father rejected her did not mean she was worthless or that other people felt the same way. She had to realize that boys would not reject her if she did not do everything they wanted her to.

If a girl has none of these personality problems and is able to meet boys, the next most common problem – and one that often brings her into conflict with her parents – is when to start going out with boys. Parents and girls alike have often asked me anxiously about the proper time to begin. The only answer seems too simple to be true – but it is. The right time is when a girl *feels* that it is the right time. Going out is, first of all, a matter of two people pairing off to get to know each other better, but in the background is the fact that one is male, the other, female, and this difference may possibly lead to some sort of physical contact and some kind of emotional relationship based on feelings that are more than friendship.

By 'the right time', then, I mean the time when a girl thinks she is ready to develop a boy-girl relationship which has potentialities. For the boy, these potentialities are much more specifically sexual : kissing, petting, even intercourse. For the girl, it means the possibility of being liked and accepted – singled out as a special person. To a girl, moreover, a boy-friend has a special meaning because he is someone interested enough in her to take her out. This gives her a sense of her own importance, a sense of status.

The beginning of going out, as I have said, may be the beginning of a conflict with parents. That conflict rises because, at the time when a girl feels she is ready to go out, the chances are that her parents think it is too early. Then she faces the problem of either disobeying her parents or not having a boy-friend until they permit it.

It helps, I think, for all girls to realize first that what they are going through is an inevitable part of growing up, and it is hard on both parents and children. If they think about the conflict with their parents hard enough, it should be clear to them that the real issue is responsibility. Parents want to feel that their children are going to behave responsibly when they are away from home in a new situation. If a girl shows that she is responsible in smaller things, perhaps there will be less objection to her beginning to go out.

If it is impossible to discuss the whole thing sensibly with parents, or if they are simply adamant about it, a good many girls will go out with boys anyway – and under the worst circumstances, because they will have to sneak around and lie about it instead of enjoying this new experience easily and naturally. It may be the first time a girl really faces the whole question of being honest with parents, about something fundamental. I can only hope that a girl in this situation will examine her own set of values carefully and try to decide whether it is more important to her to be honest with her parents or do what the other girls are doing. Unfortunately, both courses have their drawbacks, and she will have to face these honestly, too.

It comes down to a question of obeying parents and giving up temporarily some of the things one wants to do – things the other girls are doing – or going ahead and subsequently suffering guilt feelings, with the fear of getting caught in the back of her mind. Sometimes a girl is farther ahead in the end by asserting her independence and refusing to go along with the others simply because 'everybody's doing it'. In the situation I've been talking about, that kind of independence won't permit you to start having boy-friends, but it may earn you some respect and admiration from your contemporaries.

Girls who are having problems with their parents over going out or over boy-friends are in need of some older person they can talk to – not someone who is going to moralize or judge them, or give them advice, but someone who will just listen and understand. It is a lucky girl who has parents who can do this much for her. Sometimes a teacher can help, or a school counsellor, or a loved relative. I am not suggesting that the older person, whoever it is, is wiser or 'knows better.' I am only saying that such a person, by listening sympathetically, helps the girl to clarify the problem in her own mind. It's another way of helping her feel better about herself.

Let's assume now that you don't have any of the problems I have been talking about. You are already happily going out with boys. The next large cloud to loom up on the horizon is likely to be whether or not to go steady. I don't have to add that there are a great many conflicting ideas about this problem, too. If there is one aspect of a girl's sexual and social development where advice is not lacking, this is it. Actually, there is something to be said on both sides. If one argues on the side of going steady, it is easy to mention the security involved – wherever a girl wants to go, she always has a date and no lonely evenings. Then there is the undeniable fact that going steady permits a deeper emotional relationship to develop between two people than does 'playing the field', and, of course, that is a good preparation for marriage.

But there is something to be said against steady dating, too. If a girl goes out with a good many boys, she will have a better opportunity of finding out what kind of male she wants to live with eventually, what personality traits in a boy attract her and which ones make her unhappy. She may find out that moody, irritable boys don't suit her easygoing, essentially optimistic way of living. Or that boys with sharp tempers frighten her. Or that sloppy boys get on her nerves if her inclination is towards neatness – or, for that matter, the other way around. She will be able to see clearly the difference between an uncaring person and one who is warm and loving. Even if she doesn't marry the one she likes best at this age, it will help her to make up her mind later on, if she marries, or it will save her from bad, risky, emotional situations with men she meets in later life.

Not that people tend to marry those who are best for them, by any means. There are many girls who have a kind of reverse talent for this kind of thing. But more often than not, early experiences affect the eventual choice of deep relationships, whether marriage results or not.

Another advantage of not going steady is that a girl finds herself in a far greater variety of social situations, meeting new adults, making more new friends, and this is good experience in learning how to construct a satisfactory social life, besides being satisfying in itself.

There is one real danger in going steady. I am sure every girl who reads this has heard it said, but it bears repeating. In our society, many of those who begin going steady early end up by marrying either while they are still in high school or just after they leave. Ten years later, or so, both girls and boys in these marriages often wake up with the realization that there are a lot of other people in the world and a great many other experiences, sexual and otherwise, they have missed by settling so early for one person. A good part of the precious freedom which is the property of the young is gone and will not come back. These young couples, still in their early twenties and usually with one or more children, feel themselves trapped, perhaps more often than not, and a good many want desperately to get themselves untrapped, as the divorce statistics show.

The pattern that seems to be most common is neither going steady exclusively nor playing the field to the limit, but rather periods of steady, close friendships with one person followed by going out with several boys.

As far as the actual dates themselves are concerned, the chief questions which arise are those of behaviour. Here the difference between the sexes I have already mentioned becomes most important. Girls are more concerned with their reputations than boys are, and how far they go in petting, for example, is determined more by what they think the boy is going to tell other boys than by anything else.

When a boy starts to kiss a girl, her reaction is not usually to think, 'Isn't this fun? What have I been waiting for?' but 'I wonder what he'll think about me,' and 'Will he tell the other boys and what will *they* think?' It is too bad, in my opinion, that our social system is built the way it is, so that this is the kind of reaction a kiss produces, but it is one of those facts of life from which there is no escape. As long as it is necessary to play the ridiculous game of 'good girl', 'bad girl' and 'prude', I suppose the best thing a girl can do is confront squarely the kind of face she wants to present to the world and develop her behaviour accordingly. In this way a girl may not get involved in sexual situations before she is emotionally ready for them. It would make more sense, I believe, for a girl to decide rationally how far she wants to go in a particular situation with a particular boy than to be constantly concerned about her reputation. It must be recognized, however, that when a girl is emotionally involved in a situation it is extremely difficult to be rational. I can only point out that the problem exists and that it has no easy solution. It's something for a girl to think about.

There certainly should be a better reason than concern over a reputation to guide a girl in how far she ought to go with petting. Some girls go farther than they want to because they're afraid their boy-friend will tell other boys that they are 'frigid' or 'prudish'.

Earlier in the chapter I talked about what a handicap it was for a girl who wanted to go out with boys to be involved in her own problems. Concentrating on 'reputation' can be in the same category. It is important for a girl to allow herself the *freedom* to be interested in what interests her boyfriend, and this can be done only if she is free of her own hangups. There's a familiar gagline that goes, 'Let's talk about *you* for a while. What do you think of me?' There are far too many girls who behave just like that. It is the sort of thing a girl should never, never do when out with a boy. She should carefully avoid such subjects as the state of her health, the problems she has with her hair, her experiences with other boys, and – well, any girl can add to that list. Boys could make it even longer.

It is a problem of communicating, of an individual's ability to express his own feelings, whether positive or negative, and one's ability to respond to the feelings others express. But communicating means more than just talking. For example, a girl can *talk* about a coming school dance, but she *communicates* her feelings about going to it. Communicating feelings is more dangerous, because a girl makes herself more vulnerable, more open. Yet a good relationship with another person involves this very openness and this very danger. The kind of communication I am talking about has to be honest and sincere, without worrying about its effect on the other person. In short, a girl should be herself – natural, open, not exclusively concerned with making an impression on others.

In this respect, girls can help boys. Boys need to understand the role they ought to play in boy-girl relationships – as much as or more than the girls. There are all kinds of small social gestures that go with being a male or a female in our society, and these days boys are likely to forget them. They have seen too many anti-hero, tough-guy films. I mean things like helping a girl on with her coat, or opening a car door, or carrying her books. It isn't a question of right or wrong, or what is etiquette and what isn't. A girl who subtly, by her actions, encourages a boy to remember these little things is emphasizing in another way the boy-girl relationship, and that is what it is all about. By helping a boy-friend observe these ancient customs, a girl helps to develop the male-female bond between them she wants to establish.

Another complication in going out – and it can be a serious one – is the problem of age differences. Girls often want to know how much older a boy can be and still be an acceptable boy-friend. Obviously there is no simple answer. A boy's actual age, for example, may be far different from his emotional age. Then, too, a girl often finds it gratifying to have the attention of an older boy, or even a man, because that sort of attention makes her feel more special.

Consider, for instance, a thirteen- or fourteen-year-old girl who is going out with a much older boy in high school. This can be a worthwhile relationship if it is based on common interests and mutual attraction. However, it will help a girl and perhaps save her from trouble if she asks herself what other reasons the older boy might have for going out with her. Is he emotionally mature? Is he thinking of her only as a possible sexual conquest because she is exceptionally attractive even though she is so much younger? If the answer to any of these questions is yes, a girl may want to reconsider seeing him, in spite of being excited about the flattering attention she is getting.

As the age difference increases, the problems increase. Here is the same girl, but this time she is dating a twenty-one-year-old boy, home from college on vacation perhaps, or out of college and working. Again, it is possible for two such people to have a good and meaningful relationship, but now the odds are more heavily against it. The same questions ought to be asked, particularly the one about his emotional maturity.

There is an even longer step our hypothetical fourteen-year-old girl can take, and this would apply equally to girls of fifteen, sixteen or seventeen. She may be going out with the thirty-five-year-old father of the child for whom she baby-sits. It is possible that even this relationship could be a positive one, but the odds are so heavily against its turning out to be anything but disastrous that nothing can really be hoped from it except unhappiness. True, it may be exciting and fun to be noticed by such a man. But to generalize about it, the greater the age difference, the greater is the chance that the older man has some psychological problem. Almost invariably a girl's interests will be different, and the relationship is virtually certain to end badly.

Going out with married men of any age, and particularly falling in love with one, is an invitation to trouble and heartbreak. A girl must realize that, no matter what he may tell her or how convincingly he says it, the odds are at least a thousand to one that he will not divorce his wife and marry her. Neither his unhappiness at home nor his love for the girl are likely to be decisive factors when the crunch comes, as it inevitably does. To go through the sheer agony of divorce, sometimes with the wife fighting it, is too much for a man to contemplate. This is something his teenage girl-friend will not understand.

A girl who finds herself in this situation should not deceive herself about the outcome or about the man involved. If she is willing to put up with empty weekends, surreptitious meetings, and be content with having only part of a man, then she is entitled to whatever short-changed satisfaction she can get, one supposes. I know that each individual situation is special and different. The girl who is going out with a married man firmly believes that, in her case, the odds are much more in her favour than they really are. But if she is able to stop deceiving herself long enough to examine her situation honestly, she may discover that things are not at all as she thought. Often, if she is able to talk openly and freely to someone who is not directly involved with her life, it will help her see the situation more clearly.

I suppose that the question a counsellor hears most frequently from very young girls, is the plaintive query: 'How do I know I'm in love?'

First, love is not sex. They are separate things. A girl loves her parents, her dog or her best friend without the involvement of sex. Conversely, it is possible to have sex with someone without loving him. Many times love and sexual feelings are part of the same response, and when this combination occurs, it can be one of the most profound and meaningful experiences human beings are capable of having. Being 'in love' is not something distinct and separate from being 'not in love'. If we put love on a scale, the range would be from zero to a hundred. At one end somewhere would be the feelings a girl has for a boy she likes and sometimes goes out with. As she knows him better and they see each other more often, her feelings move upward on the scale, until the time comes when she feels warm and excited to be with him, wants to be with him as much as possible, and would rather be with him than with anyone else. At that point, a girl could say with some confidence, 'I am in love.' That doesn't mean she has reached the opposite end of the scale. There is a distance to go, and since love is not exactly a fixed and stable emotion, she may go up and down the scale for a time. Affection may be followed by sexual feelings and a depth of emotion far from what it was at the beginning. If it was 'calf love', it would never have gone so far. That comes quickly and goes quickly, no matter how painful it may seem at the time.

At the far end of the scale is love, real love, solid and unmistakable. It is based on trust, understanding, consideration and open communication, and it is very much worth having. I have been talking in these pages about the sexual aspects of a girl's life, because that is what the book is about, but I hope no reader will underestimate the importance of love, or fail to see that sex is only one of the many faces of love. It is possible to have sex without love and love without sex, but it is the blending of the two that produces one of the most satisfying and rewarding of human experiences. A girl's sexual feelings for a boy may not lead to intercourse, until the time she believes it is appropriate, but they become important only as they reinforce her total feeling of commitment, trust and understanding – in a word, love.

5
Petting

IN different age groups and in different parts of the country, petting has different meanings. Kissing or tongue-kissing (also called 'soul-kissing' and the 'French kiss') is often thought of as petting. In other groups and places, some touching of the sex organ has to take place before it is called 'petting'. My definition is that any physical contact of a sexual nature is petting.

To describe petting further, let me add that I believe it is a way of communicating one's sexual feelings to another person. But unless it is mutual, there can be nothing very meaningful about it. It may be best, then, to discourage petting if a girl feels she cannot accept the feeling a boy is trying to communicate to her. She should understand, too, that a boy may be so aroused himself that he forgets about her response and doesn't care whether she is responding or not. That is the time to cut it off, but gently, diplomatically. A girl ought to remember that petting, while it involves (or should involve) some degree of affection and emotional feeling, as well as interest in and appreciation of the other person, is also a prelude to intercourse. Almost all intercourse is preceded by it. That implication is always there in petting, and a girl should govern herself accordingly.

Petting itself has a progression, from one step to another, which is one of its advantages as a learning process, because progress can be stopped at any point. At its simplest, it consists of warmly embracing someone -- the hug, one of the oldest and most universal of human gestures.

This is a common demonstration of affection in our society, perhaps the most common. If petting follows, however, the next step is kissing. A girl who has never kissed a boy finds these first kisses a little awkward and probably not very exciting. When she is old enough and ready enough to be aroused, excitement will make her lips go soft and open, so that the next step inevitably occurs – tongue-kissing. From there petting proceeds, usually, to the boy's putting a hand on a girl's breast outside her clothing, then inside, and then perhaps to touching his mouth to the breast. It is only a short step from here to putting the hands on the sex organ outside the clothing, on the part of one or both, and then inside. Sometimes a boy puts his mouth on the vulva of a girl, she puts her mouth on his penis, or they may do this at the same time. But that is most likely to occur just before intercourse, if this is to be the end result of the petting session, although it can also happen by itself.

A girl may draw the line at any point in this progression, as I have said, but these are things most people do before marriage whether they have intercourse or not.

There are several advantages to petting. First, of course, it is a pleasurable experience which creates delightful body sensations and can lead to orgasm (see Chapter 6). It is, quite simply, a wonderful feeling, enjoyed by people everywhere in the world. Another advantage is that there is no possibility of pregnancy except in those extremely rare cases where the boy ejaculates at the opening of the vagina and the sperm work their way through the entire length of the vagina and up into the uterus. Still another advantage is that the possibility of communicating venereal disease is equally remote.

One of the greatest advantages, as I have indicated, is the usefulness of petting as a learning experience for marriage; it is better than intercourse itself. A boy ought to know how to stimulate a girl properly, and she ought to know what it is like to be stimulated. This stimulation is learned through the techniques of petting. Because petting embraces a whole variety of contacts, from kissing to mouth-genital contact, it can be learned in gradual steps. Each new one can be assimilated and become part of a girl's emotional knowledge, of herself and of boys. Some people have argued that petting is harmful because a girl may become fixed at this level and cannot enjoy intercourse later, but that is not likely to be true unless there are psychological problems which keep a girl from enjoying intercourse. These problems are not caused by the petting experience.

There is one disadvantage that ought to be mentioned. It is the fact that society has a certain amount of disapproval of petting, and as a result of this, it is possible that the girl's reputation may be damaged. Ordinarily the amount of petting a girl does depends to a large extent on what is accepted among her friends.

As I have indicated, a girl may not particularly like petting when she first begins and will naturally go very slowly. In the ordinary course of events, however, she learns to like it as she progresses from one step to another. Here she must remember that the boy will want to go much faster than she does, and she will have to make him slow down so that she can keep up. Sometimes it will help if she simply explains this to him in a gentle way; if he cares enough about her as a person, he will respect her feelings.

Girls discover quickly that boys want to pet them and will go as far in the process as they are permitted. Some girls use this fact, unconsciously or consciously, as a kind of lever for bargaining with a boy. If he has been particularly attentive or has taken her to an especially nice place, she may allow him to go farther than she would permit him to otherwise. But if she feels that she has been short-changed on the date, she may refuse him anything more than a good-night kiss, if that. 'What does he expect for a lousy Wimpy and a cup of coffee?' is the familiar cry. That, in my opinion, is exactly the wrong approach to petting. It is not an exchange of favours – 'I'll give you something, in proportion to what you do for me.' It is an exchange of mutual feelings, in which nothing else ought to be involved.

Sometimes, if a girl happens to be feeling hostile or irritated about something, she may deliberately let the boy get aroused in a petting situation and then refuse to continue, as a means of punishing him. It isn't hard to understand that using sex this way, as a weapon, is not only obviously unfair but closes off the kind of open communication that makes a relationship desirable.

Because it is difficult for a girl to understand how much more sexually oriented boys are than she is, she may often, without having any understanding of what she is doing, say or do provocative things that will be constantly frustrating to a boy, particularly if petting does not follow. Sometimes it is only a matter of vocabulary, of double meanings not intended. For example, a girl may say at the end of a date, 'My parents are in bed. Come on in and we'll have a good time.' By that she may mean nothing more than listening to some music and having something to eat without parents being around. Most likely, however, a boy will interpret her casual remark as, 'The coast is clear and we can pet.' Then he finds that what he thinks is an open invitation is something else, and the girl is shocked by his advances and resists them. The result: he is left irritated and frustrated because he has picked up the wrong cues.

Again, after a long kiss during petting, a girl might say, 'Wow, I'm hot!' The boy interprets this as, 'I'm all aroused and ready to go,' and takes the next step, or tries to. But the girl may have meant she was warm and beginning to perspire, and it won't occur to her that anyone would misinterpret her literal way of expressing herself. It would help girls if they could keep in mind constantly how much more sexually oriented boys are and that remarks they make will usually be interpreted in that way.

Boys have a short, descriptive word for girls who deliberately get them worked up and then back off, leaving them frustrated. The word is 'cock-teaser'. You may think it a shocking, ugly word (parents probably will, although they knew it well when they were growing up), but it accurately describes a practice which is not only clearly unfair but tells us something about the personality of the girl who does it. Such behaviour may be unconscious with some girls. They don't understand what they are doing or what effect it will have, because of their inexperience or ignorance, and they are surprised and indignant when a boy responds aggressively to being treated that way. If matters are explained to such a girl and she understands what has happened, she will be much better able to decide what she wants to do about petting.

Another kind of girl, however, is a different proposition. She knows perfectly well what she is doing and does it out of malice, spite or resentment. She is an actress playing the lead role in a drama of hostility because, for deepseated and complicated reasons, she doesn't like males in general and chooses this way to get even with them. A few tease for a different reason. Other girls have convinced them that it is the smart thing to do and may even show them how to do it. Then there are those who want to dominate males and tease because it is a way of controlling boys and showing aggression. Such a girl may well have deep psychological problems which will show up later in marriage, and consequently she ought to work them out while she is still adolescent, perhaps with professional help either through her own doctor or from a Youth Advisory Centre such as those run by the Family Planning Association and some Local Health Authorities.

From all of this I hope no one will believe I am implying that girls are essentially 'cold fish' and that they are less responsive sexually. In fact, about a third of them are as sexually responsive as the average male.

As I will point out in the following chapter, girls who have orgasm when they are young are the ones who have the easiest time in making a good sexual adjustment in marriage. Of all the ways to have an orgasm, petting to that point is probably the most helpful. If a girl becomes aroused sexually in petting, however, and then does not have an orgasm, she often feels frustrated and unsatisfied. If this occurs over and over again, it builds up habit patterns difficult to break after she is married or as she gets older. Sometimes, too, petting without orgasm leaves her with pains in her groin that can be very uncomfortable. About half of the girls who are aroused during petting have that experience, and about a third of them masturbate afterwards to relieve tension. Either continuing to pet until orgasm occurs or masturbating later are certainly better than living with this frustration and uneasiness.

After so much talk about petting, I should add that one ought to be careful, parents especially, not to overemphasize it. Parents are likely to believe that the younger generation today is 'wild', to use the terminology of their generation. But in spite of all that is said and written about free sexual behaviour among adolescents, there are still a large number of girls who have not petted at all by the time they finish high school. Not surprisingly, the majority of girls have not started to pet by the time they are thirteen or fourteen. Almost without exception, however, girls pet before marriage, at some time or other, and petting to orgasm is more common with the new generation. For many girls it solves the problem of not having intercourse yet still learning to respond sexually to the male, which is an important thing to learn. Petting and self-masturbation are probably the most acceptable kinds of sexual behaviour among adolescent girls.

If there is little more actual sexual behaviour in this generation than in the previous one, it is true that they drink alcohol a good deal, and the use of drugs has now become a national problem. Without going into other aspects of this question, something needs to be said about the relationship of alcohol and drugs to sex, since they are so often considered to be closely linked.

Boys sometimes believe that alcohol is the best way to stimulate a girl to sex. They know that *they* feel more un-inhibited and amorous when they have been drinking, and think a girl feels the same way. Since they imagine themselves more alert and sensitive to every kind of stimulation when they drink, they are convinced that, with the aid of alcohol, any boy and girl can drink themselves into sex.

In a way, this is true. There is no doubt alcohol removes some inhibitions. But it is a depressant rather than a stimulant, and only a small amount (a drink or two) is necessary to depress the higher nervous centres. Some inhibition is lost, while there is an illusion of being stimulated. Then it takes only a little more to depress the lower nervous centres, with quite a different effect, because then the drinker will not be able to function as well sexually or otherwise as he was before. The more he drinks, the longer it will take a boy to have an erection and ejaculate. As for the girl, the more she drinks the less likely she will be to want sex.

In the case of drugs, it must be remembered that there are two broad categories: depressants, like alcohol, and stimulants. Marijuana, for example, is a depressant, and the popular belief that 'pot and sex' are inseparable companions is as much a delusion as the belief about alcohol. If a stimulant drug is taken – one of the amphetamines or the highly dangerous methedrine, known as 'speed' — the effect, paradoxically, is the same. Such drugs stimulate the individual every way but sexually and have a similar depressing effect on sexual behaviour. 'Main line' drugs like heroin knock out the taker sexually, and he is completely unable to perform under their influence, notwithstanding that he may have elaborate sexual fantasies.

Girls (and boys, for that matter) should understand that alcohol and drugs are like crutches, as far as sex is concerned. If a person imagines he needs them to have sex, then there is something wrong with his personality and he needs help. Sex exists, fully and beautifully, by itself without any artificial help.

6

The Female Orgasm

PERHAPS I should begin by saying that the orgasm is another one of those things women worry about unnecessarily. 'The tyranny of the orgasm', the noted novelist Mary McCarthy once called this perennial anxiety. Certainly it is nothing for young girls to worry about, since most of them will not experience it before they are fifteen. In the next five years, most of them will, one way or another, and there should be no problems about it that healthy attitudes or good counselling will not solve.

Nevertheless, girls *are* curious about the orgasm quite naturally. Their curiosity is stimulated by what they read. If there is a common denominator in their questions, it would be, 'What is it really like? How will I feel? How do I know when I'm having it?'

Many of the greatest writers of world literature have tried to answer those questions, and, of course, contemporary novels are full of less masterful descriptions. Doctors, naturally, describe its clinical aspects. Sometimes those who specialize in sexual studies are able, in a way, to combine the two. One of the most famous of these researchers, the British sexologist Havelock Ellis, whose *Studies in the Psychology of Sex* was a pioneering landmark in this field, describes orgasm achieved by intercourse as a state in which 'the individual, as a separate person, tends to disappear. He has become one with another person, as nearly one as the conditions of existence ever permit.' Describing how a woman feels when she is having orgasm, Ellis speaks of her 'feeling of relieved tension and agreeable repose – a moment when, as one woman expresses it, together with intense pleasure, there is, as it were, a floating up into a higher sphere. . . . [After the orgasm] there is a sensation of repose and self-assurance, and often an accession of free and joyous energy. . . . She may experience a feeling as of intoxication, lasting for several hours, an intoxication that is followed by no evil reaction.'

Today, research into the nature of sexual response has given us a fairly comprehensive knowledge of what happens to the body during orgasm. It can be divided into four parts, of which the orgasm itself is the third. First there is the excitement phase, beginning with a moistening of the vagina by its lubricating fluid. This moistening occurs in ten to thirty seconds from the first sexual stimulation, no matter what its source may be. Stimulation of the clitoris contributes to this phase, too, although it is not essential. The nipples on the breasts become erect, and the breasts themselves increase in size. The outer lips of the vulva, the *labia majoris*, open a little, while the inner lips also tend to swell. Apart from the sex organs, this phase is also reflected in other parts of the body, as the voluntary muscles tense, the pulse rate increases, blood pressure rises and a rosy glow called the 'sex flush' appears on the skin.

Excitement is succeeded by the plateau phase – although it would be hard to say exactly where one phase stops and the next begins. Now the rate of breathing increases, and pulse rate and blood pressure begin to rise. The sex flush becomes more marked and widespread. Muscle tension is heightened. The area around the breast nipples swells. Most dramatic, however, is the swelling of the tissues around the outer third of the vagina, so that the diameter of this third is reduced as much as fifty per cent, enabling it to grip the penis. Changes continue in the uterus and vagina, and the uterus itself is enlarged, doubling in size in women who have had children. The clitoris elevates, like a male erection, and the inner lips change in colour from pink to bright red. This colour signals that the orgasm is going to occur in a minute or a minute and a half, if stimulation continues.

Orgasm itself is the third phase. There is a feeling of intense pleasure as the outer third of the vaginal tube goes into rhythmic muscular contractions, coming four fifths of a second apart until the intensity tapers off. In a mild orgasm there may be only three to five contractions; in an intense one, eight to twelve. The uterus also contracts rhythmically, in wave-like motions like its contractions during childbirth, but these contractions are not felt. Other muscles may contract in the same way. In the rest of the body, pulse rate, blood pressure and breathing rate reach their peaks, the sex flush is pronounced and all the body's muscles respond in some way. Hands and feet contract in a spasm. Through it all, both female and male are unaware of these muscular exertions and may be surprised when some of their muscles ache the next day.

After the orgasm, a kind of final resolution occurs. The swelling around the nipples subsides, giving an illusion that the nipples themselves are more erect than ever. This appearance is a sign that a woman has really had orgasm. The sex flush disappears rapidly, and in many girls a filmy sheen of perspiration appears on the body. Within five to ten seconds, the clitoris returns to its normal position but it may take five or ten minutes or as long as a half hour to get back to normal size. The vagina relaxes, too, the uterus shrinks and the cervix descends to its normal position. At this point the passage through the cervix enlarges, which probably makes it easier for the sperm cells to swim into the uterus. It may be as long as a half hour after orgasm before a girl's entire body returns to the state it was in before she was stimulated. If she has reached the plateau stage without experiencing orgasm, it will take much longer – an hour or even several hours.

Orgasm can be a very mild experience, almost as mild as a peaceful sigh, or it can be an extreme state of ecstasy, with much threshing about, and momentary loss of awareness. It can last for a very few seconds or for thirty seconds and longer. There is, in brief, no right or wrong way to have an orgasm.

There has long been a common misconception, still prevalent even today, that there are two different kinds of orgasm, one achieved by stimulation of the clitoris, and thus called a 'clitoral orgasm' : the other, a 'vaginal orgasm', accomplished by the penis's penetration of the vagina. The first was thought to be achieved by masturbation, petting or intercourse if the male pubic area pressed against the clitoris. It was considered to be an immature kind of orgasm, related to early sexual experiences. The vaginal orgasm was believed to be more mature and to be the ultimate sexual experience for a woman.

Today we know these ideas are not true and that in intercourse it is the stimulation of the clitoris by the male area above the penis which brings on orgasm in conjunction with the pulling down of the *labia* by the action of the penis moving in and out of the vagina. This in turn stimulates the clitoris because the pulling-down action creates a hood of flesh over the sensitive tip end of the clitoris, rubbing against it.

There is, in fact, no real difference in the kind of orgasm girls have, either by masturbation, petting or intercourse. The idea that, if a girl has sex in one particular way, say masturbation, it will prevent her from having orgasm in intercourse is simply not true.

Whatever its duration or intensity, the orgasm is a unique and specific enough experience so that when a girl has one, she can be in no doubt that she is having it. In a sense, it is like a much more familiar bodily function, the sneeze. After reading the description of orgasm I have given here, if a girl still has doubts about whether she has had one or not, the chances are good that she has not.

There are several sources of orgasm. For young girls up to fifteen, most orgasms are produced (in those who have them) by self-masturbation. I shall have more to say about that in a later chapter. Dreams are another source, but only about two girls out of a hundred achieve orgasm that way at fifteen; by twenty, this figure increases to eight out of a hundred. At fifteen, three girls out of a hundred have orgasm by petting to climax, but again a dramatic change occurs in the next five years. At twenty, nearly twenty-five per cent of girls who have orgasm achieve it this way. Only six per cent of girls have had orgasm from intercourse at fifteen; from sixteen to twenty, this figure rises to eleven per cent. An even smaller percentage, two per cent, have had orgasm with other girls at fifteen, and at twenty this figure has risen by only a single percentage point.

Quite naturally, as a girl gets older the frequency of orgasm achieved through masturbation decreases while the frequency of orgasm from petting and intercourse rises.

All this may sound to some girls as though everybody is engaged in some kind of sexual activity all the time, and those who have never experienced orgasm may well be wondering why so much fuss is made about it. After all, they reason, it may be a pleasurable experience to be enjoyed later, but they see no reason to get upset because they are not having it now. This is understandable. Yet there *is* something to be said for those who do. The longer a girl delays having orgasm, whatever the source, the more difficult it may be to have it in later life because of the steady build-up of inhibition in the meantime.

Some parents may not like to hear such things, but it is demonstrably true that girls who have orgasm when they are young – that is, up to fifteen – are those who have the least difficulty having one in marriage later on. It doesn't matter whether the orgasm comes from intercourse, petting or masturbation, as far as this ability is concerned. Half the girls who have never had an orgasm before marriage fail to have one during the first year of marriage, but of those who have experienced it, only one in ten fails to have it during the first marital year. Surprisingly, girls who have intercourse when they are young but do not experience orgasm have just as hard a time, or harder, having it after marriage.

One superstition that needs to be discarded is the idea, earnestly believed by some people, that if a girl learns to have an orgasm by masturbating herself or having someone do it to her, she will be so accustomed to this method of achieving it that she will have trouble experiencing it in intercourse. There is no truth whatever in this notion. In fact, it is easier to transfer the way you achieve orgasm from one kind of sexual behaviour to another than it is to have one in the first place.

One advantage girls have over boys where the orgasm is concerned is their ability to have many of them in succession. Some young boys are able to have three or four in relatively quick succession, with a short interval between, but they lose this ability progressively as they grow older. Many girls, on the other hand, from the time they begin to have them until the time they cease sexual activity, are able to have almost an unlimited number in succession. Not every girl does this, of course. There is tremendous variation here, as there is in every other area of sexual activity. Some girls are satisfied with one, some cannot keep themselves from having many. The statistics show that one or two girls out of every ten have more than one orgasm.

The second orgasm occurs sometimes almost immediately after the first, while the girl is still much aroused and has not come down from her orgasmic peak, or it can occur after she does come down, then builds up to a new peak, twenty or thirty minutes later. For some girls, these multiple orgasms may peak ten, thirty or fifty times in the course of one sex experience. Very often in such a long series the peaks are smaller, but each one can be just as satisfying as it is to the woman who has only one.

In spite of all a girl may hear to the contrary, especially about the mythical trouble known as 'nymphomania', there is nothing 'abnormal' about having more than one orgasm. Most women could have several at a time if they really tried. A 'nymphomaniac' has been defined as a woman who cannot be satisfied sexually. She is constantly excited and, whether she has orgasm or not, wants to have more and more sex. This notion was invented by males, and it is an exciting idea for them. It is only an idea, however, in my opinion, and does not actually exist in real life. If I had to define a 'nymphomaniac', I would say that she is a woman who has a higher rate of sexual outlet than the person who calls her that name. If a girl's sexual response is high and constant, there is no reason for her to worry that she is a 'nymphomaniac'. Rather, she should be pleased that she *is* so responsive, and she will find that she is closer to males in her sexual response.

Another idea that needs to be brought into better focus is the notion that it is highly desirable if both partners in the sex act have orgasm at the same time. This is splendid if it happens, but it isn't that important. The intercourse will be pleasurable in any case, under ordinary circumstances. If they cannot wait for each other, then the one who achieves orgasm first helps the one who is late to come to climax. It *is* important for the partner who hasn't had the orgasm to have one. That may require more intercourse or petting until he or she does.

Nevertheless, in the sex act itself, whether it is petting or intercourse, it is still necessary for each partner to be self-centred for the time being, enough to achieve his own pleasure because, paradoxically, this is the very thing which will bring most pleasure to the other partner.

Even if orgasm is not achieved, however, either partner can get a great deal of pleasure out of sex simply from the pleasure he gives. Consequently, even though the orgasm is a highly enjoyable experience, it isn't the extent of the good feelings a man or a woman can have from sex. The feeling of closeness, the shared pleasure, the blissful intimacy of people who love each other – all these have such definite positive values that the orgasm itself should never be viewed as a tyrant, without which the whole act is meaningless.

The girl who has never had an orgasm may be disappointed because she doesn't automatically have one the first time she tries to achieve it by masturbation, petting or intercourse. It is something like learning to play tennis or the piano. It is necessary to learn, through practice, how to build up to this peak. For some girls it is easier than for others. There are those who take months or years to learn it well. Others achieve it satisfactorily the first time they try. It is a learning process, like any other.

7

Intercourse

ONE of the most frequent non-political arguments to be heard today is the continuing discussion of whether or not young people should have premarital intercourse. My own feeling is that this question is not nearly so important as it is made out to be. I see no magic in the fact of a penis entering a vagina, either in terms of curing the ills of the world or bringing about its downfall. A far more important question, it seems to me, is what sort of relationship with each other two people are able to develop, and that includes the kind of sexual adjustment they can make.

Strangely enough, when people talk about 'premarital sex' or 'sex relations' or 'sleeping with' someone, they usually mean premarital intercourse, but it is quite possible to have premarital sex or to sleep with someone without any intercourse whatever.

Girls and boys have different attitudes to intercourse and its meaning. To many boys it is a conquest – accomplishing something, imposing their desires on a girl, accompanied by a feeling of exaltation. Most girls do not have this feeling. Instead, they think of it as giving in, accepting, or permitting the male to become victorious. In earlier days, these differences between males and females were so sharp in degree that a girl was expected to lie down and take whatever the male chose to give her. This is no longer true, of course. Now a girl is, or can be if she chooses, an equal partner in intercourse, enjoying it, taking part in it actively, being aggressive about it if she feels like it. Even with the newer equality, however, it is still true that intercourse has a somewhat different meaning for a girl. Maybe it is because of the psychological feelings rising from the fact that she is the one being penetrated, and the male is doing the penetrating.

A girl should consider both sides of this question carefully if she comes to a point where she thinks she is going to have to make up her mind about it – and consider it calmly, before emotion pushes her into a decision she might have been better prepared to make if she had thought about all the alternatives, pro and con.

Here are some reasons which might make a girl think favourably of having premarital intercourse :

1. It seems so obvious, but there are people who don't understand that the chief reason for having intercourse, aside from the desire to have a baby, is that it is one of the most delightful, exciting and stimulating experiences a human being can know. It is no harder to understand wanting to have intercourse than it is to understand the urge to play tennis, swim, dance, ride a horse, or to do anything else that gives us pleasure.

Unfortunately, this simple, straightforward reason has to be qualified by remembering that much of the pleasure will be lost if intercourse is accompanied by strong guilt feelings about it. Girls, too, ought to be wary (romantic as they are) of glorifying intercourse before they have had it. Everything they read, or see on the screen, or hear about from older girls, leads them to believe that intercourse is the ultimate in human satisfactions, something almost indescribable. Then they have it and often they are disappointed to find that the world doesn't necessarily stop, or the 'earth move', as Hemingway put it in *For Whom the Bell Tolls*. The ringing of bells may not drown out every other sound, or the night sky of the mind light up with flashing rockets. Having anticipated vaguely so much more than the experience can give, they may be quite disillusioned and inquire, 'Is this all there is to it? Is this what the shouting is about?' It may seem no more to such girls than a feeling like that of masturbation, only heightened by the presence of another person.

Girls who are more reasonable in their expectations are clearly more likely to find intercourse enjoyable. The trouble is that because society, and especially parents, are so upset and adamant about the very idea of premarital intercourse, girls who have never had it get the idea that it must be incredibly wonderful if it is so forbidden. Intercourse is an important and permanent part of most people's lives. It is a wise idea to get it into perspective from the beginning.

2. As I have indicated, premarital intercourse can also be a training ground for marriage. Those who have had it have been given some valuable lessons in learning to live with someone else in what Bernard Shaw called 'the dreadful intimacy of marriage'. The lessons are valuable, that is, if intercourse is performed with good techniques, if it is meaningful to the people involved, if it is part of a whole relationship, and if it is done without feelings of guilt and fear. What is done badly, however, may be carried over into marriage. It is somewhat like learning to play tennis and discovering when you face someone across the net in your first real match that you haven't learned the fundamentals properly.

3. Another reason for premarital intercourse is the fact that, unlike masturbation, it means interaction with another human being and consequently is a means of learning how to live with people, something everyone has to do. Because this is true, it is important that the intercourse be a giving-and-receiving act.

There are many girls – I have no idea what the percentage is – who regret after marriage that they didn't have premarital intercourse, because they have come to realize what a long, slow learning process it is after marriage. Sometimes, too late, they and their husbands discover they are not suited to each other sexually.

4. If the premarital intercourse is with a boy a girl expects to marry, it is a good way for her to find out if she is going to enjoy the constant intimacy of the bedroom with that particular young man, and, of course, it gives him the same opportunity. A girl should not forget that in many marriages the partners are suited to each other in every way but sexually, and if one discovers this fact *after* marriage, the only result can be trouble. Finding out before, however, must be a fair test. The intercourse would have to be done in the most relaxed circumstances. If it has to be done with strong guilt feelings or furtively and hastily, it isn't like being married and so it is not a fair test.

5. People learn more easily when they are young. If the learning is correct from the beginning, sexual adjustment in marriage is made much more easily.

6. Some girls have premarital intercourse because all their friends, or most of them, are having it and they will lose status in the group if they don't. This is a powerful pressure, but it isn't necessarily a good one. I shall talk about that presently, in considering the 'cons'.

What *are* the cons, then?

1. First, and most obvious, the danger of pregnancy. In this era of 'the pill', a good deal of that danger has been removed for those with access to a contraceptive like the pill. But young, adolescent girls are not likely to have that opportunity and so pregnancy becomes a real and present danger. I will be discussing contraceptives a little later on, but let me say here that, if they are used correctly, the possibility of pregnancy is virtually eliminated.

2. Another danger is venereal disease, a subject I will

also talk about later, but again it is worth noting here that this danger has also decreased because of modern drugs – venereal disease yields to drugs with relative ease if it is treated promptly by a doctor.

3. Premarital intercourse sometimes results in a forced marriage, and that is usually a poor way to enter the married state. Some people might have married each other in any case, but more often the girl (or boy) who has been compelled to marry has a more difficult time making the marriage work, and the percentage of failure is high.

4. If there is guilt, there is likely to be damage of some kind, and in my opinion this is the most important reason for not having premarital intercourse. Guilt is determined by the attitude each person has towards the act, and it is better not to have intercourse at all if one (or both persons) feels extremely guilty and is likely to suffer attacks of conscience afterwards.

5. Girls often are afraid a boy will lose respect for them if they have intercourse with him, and there is no doubt this sometimes happens. A girl ought to ask herself if she honestly believes a boy is more concerned about her as an individual, as a whole person, than he is with one particular part of her, the vagina. The whole question of virginity is involved here, too – another subject I shall get to presently.

6. A less pressing danger of premarital intercourse is the possibility that *after* marriage guilt feelings about it will be stirred up. That rarely happens, however. It is less likely to happen the more intercourse there is before marriage.

7. Guilt about premarital intercourse is often the result of fear about what happens to those who get caught. The worst that happens is public disapproval – from school, parents, clergy, police, relatives, even friends. People are not often caught, however, and if they are, how they feel about it depends a great deal on who catches them. Worst, quite naturally, is to have disapproving parents find out. If

it is a friend or someone their own age, the result is usually no more than feelings of embarrassment.

The responsible couple who have weighed the pros and cons and decided to have intercourse must accept the risks involved. But just as they learn to 'drive defensively' in driving lessons, they should minimize the risk in a realistic way.

8. A very real danger of premarital intercourse is the possibility that it may result in overemphasizing the physical side of a relationship. If that seems probable, a girl would be better off not to have it. The value of premarital sex is that it becomes an important part of a whole relationship between people, not an isolated experience. If a girl thinks a boy only wants to 'get off' with her in this sense rather than to have a whole relationship, she may discover that she has a sexual partner but not a friend.

9. It should not be overlooked that to many people, and probably to more girls than boys, premarital intercourse is morally wrong. In the past it was thought to be wrong for girls, but men's behaviour was winked at, and the phrase 'sowing his wild oats' was coined to describe it. The new equality of the sexes, however, means that girls are entitled to equal responsibilities and opportunities in sexual as well as other areas of living. Something that is morally wrong for a girl ought to be just as wrong for a boy.

In the end the problem of premarital sex comes down to a question of how a girl feels about it, whether she thinks it is right or wrong. When a girl thinks it is wrong, none of the reasons for having it I have mentioned will make the slightest difference to her. If she believes it is not wrong, her responsibility then is to think carefully about the time, the place and the partner. There is always the danger that, because the sex impulse is so powerful, a girl will be carried away without assessing rights or wrongs, or without being as sure as she can be about her partner's attitudes. I hope that being forewarned by the information given here will make her forearmed.

For the sake of further information, let us assume that a girl has decided to have intercourse. Quite often she doesn't know what to expect or what to do, and the experience is a fumbling and unsatisfactory one. For instance, if she has seen an erect male penis, she may be frightened by the thought of such a large object penetrating her and wonders how it is possible. A little knowledge of her own anatomy, as described in Chapter 2, will be helpful here. What seems like a mere slit at the opening of the vagina is actually, as I have noted, an opening of amazing flexibility, as it would have to be to make the birth of a baby possible. Remembering that will take away the fear of its being stretched painfully by the relatively small mass of a penis. Moreover, when a girl is aroused, the lubrication of the vagina which results makes insertion of the penis easy. Intercourse is more comfortable, consequently, when it has been preceded by sex play.

As for intercourse itself, the position for it in our culture is by tradition for the girl to lie on her back with her legs apart, while the boy lies on her, face to face, with his legs together. A girl sometimes will help him to insert his penis, but more often he will do it by himself. Usually the insertion is made gradually, with small thrusts forward.

If a girl is a virgin, the hymen will be broken by the penetration, with a quick, sharp pain that is soon over, and a little bleeding, which is not at all serious. That is the usual way of things. But when the hymen happens to be tougher and the boy has to push with more force to break it, there may be more pain and discomfort, and quite possibly a girl may not enjoy this first intercourse for that reason. Its satisfactions will come in succeeding intercourse. The danger here is that a girl who is unprepared for this possibility may find sex distasteful and take a long time to get over the unpleasantness of the first experience. This psychological damage can be prevented, or at least minimized, if a boy pets a girl a good deal first and inserts his fingers in her vagina.

Once penetrated, the vagina clasps the penis in a velvet grip and intercourse continues with a series of pelvic thrusts. These increase in speed, frequency and force as excitement mounts and the act moves towards orgasm, as I described earlier. Sometimes the male ejaculates too quickly, before a girl can have her own orgasm. There are measures a boy can take for himself to prevent this, but what a girl can do on her own behalf is to slow down her partner by insisting on more petting before penetration begins, so that she will be farther along the road towards orgasm.

There are other positions for intercourse, employed either for the sake of variety or because it helps the male to slow down and the female to speed up. This is best accomplished by the position in which the female lies on top of the male, with her legs together between his, or vice versa. She can help the male, and help herself, by making him put his hands on her buttocks, which pushes her pelvic area towards his and makes it easier for her to thrust and build up tension for the orgasm. The weight of her body also reduces his body movement, and that, too, will help him delay ejaculation.

In another position, the couple lie on their sides facing each other, with the girl's leg often thrown over the male's leg, permitting them to get closer together. In fact, people can have intercourse sitting down or standing up, as well, but these positions are taken more for the sake of variety.

Still another position is what is commonly called 'dog fashion', in which the girl lies on her stomach with the male over her, or on her side with him behind her, or on her back with the male beneath her. An advantage of this position is that it makes the clitoris more available for stimulation with the hand.

If a girl thinks some of these positions are strange, she should remember that they by no means represent the range of positions for intercourse when one considers the whole world. For example, people who live in some South Sea islands have a position which seems truly odd to us, in which the female lies on her back with her legs out, while the male kneels or squats in front of her to make his pelvic thrusts. There are, in fact, many ways to have intercourse and there is no 'right' or 'wrong' about it. 'Right' is what works best for the people involved, and what may seem strange to one couple is commonplace for another. Nor is there any such thing as a 'normal' position. Many people in our culture think the position in which the female lies on her back is the 'normal' one, but it is only the most common.

When intercourse is over, there is another difference between males and females. The male usually feels immediately let down and wants to withdraw and go to sleep, while the female may want more penetration and more love play. She appreciates the man who understands this and thinks of her different kind of need. A knowledgeable girl can explain this to a boy who may not know about it. A girl (or a boy) who wants to get out of bed immediately after intercourse and wash herself is probably reflecting another attitude to sex – the feeling that it is something dirty. Most likely she is not really happy about the act itself but there is nothing unclean about the body's secretions.

Love, or at least affection, is the motivation to intercourse for most girls, and so it is no wonder that they are curious about those who do it for money. Young girls often regard prostitutes with mingled fascination and horror.

They find it hard to understand how a woman could have intercourse with just *any* man. In prostitution, affection, friendship or the interchange of feelings does not often occur. Unfortunately, when there is a great deal of hostility involved in these encounters, on one or both sides, sometimes it turns out to be a depressing experience for a man. For the prostitute, the act may often be only an expression of her hatred for men, although contrary to popular belief, she may actually enjoy sex with many different men and will have orgasm with some of them.

The contrast, however, is striking. Prostitution is usually a sex act performed in a drab room somewhere, in a boarding house or a fourth-class hotel, and the sordid setting often reflects the nature of the act. The same lack of emotional content may exist, nevertheless, if the prostitute is being paid £30 or more, and the act takes place in an expensive hotel or apartment. What is important is the fact that, even when intercourse takes place between people who have only warm feelings for each other, the quality of the act may be affected by the setting. I want to emphasize this aspect of it, because it is much more important for a girl not to be interrupted or found out than it is for a boy. She is also more easily distracted by her surroundings and by small things which a boy might not even notice.

Couples who have made a decision to have intercourse need to exercise their ingenuity in finding the best place to have it, where the chances of discovery will not be great. One of the more common places, but one that can be cramped and uncomfortable, is a car parked along the road. Another is a lovers' lane or a similar secluded spot, where there is also the danger of robbery or rape, or being found by people who get a sadistic-sexual pleasure out of creeping up on parked cars. The home of either the girl or the boy is possible only if they can be absolutely certain that parents won't return home unexpectedly. If there is any doubt, anxiety and tension will almost inevitably surround the act. Motel and hotel rooms are not usually accessible to younger couples. In the end, it seems, places like woods, a beach, or a secluded area one can walk to are likely to work out better than any of the others I have mentioned.

I do not want to minimize the importance of the step a girl takes when she decides to have intercourse for the first time. It is her crossing of the Rubicon, from which there is no turning back. While it is true, as I said at the beginning, that our society makes altogether too much out of the problem of premarital intercourse, at the same time it must be remembered that it is one of the most important steps in a girl's life. The fundamental fact is that once she has had intercourse, she will never again be a virgin. Fortunately, virginity or non-virginity is more a state of mind than a condition of the body. For example, here is a fifteen-year-old girl who is warm, open, affectionate and has not developed any guilt feelings about sex. In the course of a long relationship with a boyfriend, during which there has been an increased emotional involvement with each other, along with increased petting experiences, intercourse occurs at some particular point. In this girl's mind there has been no sudden or dramatic change in her status from being a virgin to being a non-virgin. Instead, the intercourse has been only another expression of her fondness for the boy. If the relationship is broken off later and she begins a new relationship with another boy, she will not enter it with any different feelings towards herself than she had in her previous relationship.

Even though intercourse may not be the big deal it is so often made out to be, it does provide a certain completeness to a relationship. If people feel open and loving towards each other, yet erect certain barriers – no petting below the waist, or everything but intercourse – a certain restraint is bound to develop. I am not suggesting that there be no barriers. I am only saying that it is better to face these barriers consciously and understand the pros and cons of erecting them. In sex, as in every other aspect of human relationships, understanding is the glue that holds everything together.

8

Consequences

THE most obvious consequence of intercourse is pregnancy. In our society, getting pregnant before marriage is a social and economic problem so serious that most girls would do anything they could to avoid it. Moralists believe the problem can be dealt with simply by forbidding girls to have intercourse, but as everyday life shows us, this approach accomplishes very little. The number of unmarried mothers every year, especially at the secondary school level, is sufficient proof that this idea doesn't work.

It is easy for people to condemn the unmarried pregnant girl, and a good many do, but it is a far more constructive thing to help her. Some enlightened large cities do help these days by setting up schools and classes for such girls, enabling them to continue their schooling and giving them instruction in pre-natal and maternal care, with excellent results. Our society is unique in its sometimes almost savage attitude towards unmarried pregnant girls. In some other societies, it is quite acceptable to get pregnant before marriage, and there are those in which it is necessary for girls to prove their fertility by having a baby before they marry.

Nevertheless, we must accept the conditions of our own culture; consequently it is necessary to prevent pregnancy, if possible, when a couple chooses to have intercourse outside marriage. Since the early days of mankind, attempts have been made to avoid pregnancy by using some kind of contraceptive device. Today we have come a long way down that particular medical road and there is available now a wide choice of contraceptive means, although their usefulness and practicality, particularly where the young unmarried girl is concerned, are not always satisfactory.

The best kind of contraceptive available today is the birth-control pill, now used extensively and so familiar a phenomenon in British life that it is known simply as 'the pill' and its use has even inspired a Hollywood film. It prevents a woman from ovulating and consequently there is no chance for her to get pregnant because there is no egg to be fertilized. She begins taking these pills on the fifth day after her last period, counting the first day of menstruation as day one. She takes the pills, one a day, until the packet is used up, which takes twenty-one or twenty-two days, depending on the brand. She then stops for six to seven days, again depending on the brand of the pill, and then starts on a new packet for a further twenty-one or twenty-two days, after which she rests again for a week, and so on. Even though she is not taking the pill during the rest period, she can still continue to have intercourse without any fear of pregnancy. The month's supply of pills costs from 28p to 43p at a Family Planning Clinic; and from 29p to 53p at a chemist.

One of the good side effects of the pill is that a woman's menstrual periods are very light and of short duration, rarely more than three days. Also, she is not likely to have severe cramps or pain any more, if she has had these symptoms before. But there can be bad side effects, too. About five per cent of women have them. They include putting on weight, nausea, tenderness in the breast, and a feeling of being bloated. Also, for girls under sixteen, because they are still growing, the pill may have a bad effect on them.

Although there is nothing in this world that is one hundred per cent perfect, the pills are so close to it that, when they are properly used, a girl has no need to worry. Fortunately, there are eleven different variations of these pills approved by the Family Planning Association, so that, if there are side effects from using one particular brand, changing to another may eliminate these symptoms.

The pill cannot be purchased without a doctor's prescription, and there are enough complications involved with its use for it to be important to have a doctor prescribe them and to have regular checkups when they are being used. Girls over sixteen can consult any doctor independently of parental permission; it will depend on circumstances whether the doctor wants the parent to be consulted. Generally, unless there are strong medical or other reasons, general practitioners respect the wishes of their patients for the consultation to remain confidential. Any girl over the age of sixteen can also attend a Family Planning Association clinic; there is no need to get a doctor's letter first. The FPA doctor writes to the doctor of every girl for whom she prescribes the pill, so that he may say whether in his opinion there are medical reasons why this particular contraceptive method should not be used for the patient.

By all odds, the most practical method of contraception, as far as young girls are concerned, is a rubber sheath put over the penis, called a 'condom', or 'French letter'. These condoms can be bought at chemists, barbers shops and sometimes from slot machines in men's lavatories. They are supplied by the boys, naturally, if intercourse is contemplated, and that is just the trouble, because it places control of contraception in the hands of the male. Since the girl is so much more affected by pregnancy than the boy, control ought more logically to be in her hands.

Condoms have one advantage over every other kind of contraception because they prevent venereal disease, a subject we will talk about later. They are also inexpensive, costing about 3p to 15p each, and are used only once. They are not quite as safe as the pill because occasionally they may slip off during intercourse, and sometimes they tear or break if the intercourse is very active. Still, they are ninety-nine per cent effective, and if a girl is serious about not getting pregnant and is having intercourse without the pill, she should not permit a boy to insert his penis unless he is using a condom.

Human ingenuity being what it is, there are often attempts to use some kind of substitute for condoms – crude devices like rubber balloons cut to fit, or even Saranwrap. These devices are little better than no protection at all and should never be used.

A device much in use among married women is a dome-shaped vaginal cap made of rubber, known as a 'diaphragm'. It comes in different sizes, to accommodate women's varying sizes, and must be fitted by a doctor. He shows the woman how to place the diaphragm over the cervix. With a little practice, the woman learns to insert the diaphragm, first smearing it with a special cream or jelly designed to kill sperm. She must leave it in for eight hours after intercourse. For obvious reasons, this device is not suitable for young girls.

Still another contraceptive is the vaginal foam, jelly or pessary. There are many of them, and they can be bought in chemists without a doctor's prescription. They have the further advantage of being easy to use and inexpensive. Recent improvements have made some of them more dependable than they were before.

Pessaries come wrapped individually. They are about the size of an almond. Before intercourse, one is inserted into the vagina and it melts at body temperature, coating the vagina with chemicals which kill the sperm and also tend to prevent them from ascending to the organs inside. But they have definite disadvantages. They don't always melt when they should, and sometimes do not melt completely. Many women think they melt too easily and it is too messy to insert them. In this category of contraceptives, the pessary is probably the least effective, though until recently, before the pill, advertising had made it the most widely used, because women believed that pessaries advertised for feminine hygiene were good for contraception, but they are not.

Creams are also available in this category, some of them the same ones originally meant to be used with diaphragms. The companies making these creams say they are as effective without the diaphragm, and there seems to be some truth in this claim, since it is the cream that does the job, not the diaphragm, which only holds the cream in place against the opening of the uterus. Creams are inserted into the vagina with a plastic applicator, just before intercourse. Again, some women think this is a messy business and say the cream is still leaking out next day in the form of a discharge.

Among these chemical products, perhaps the best are the new contraceptive foams. Messiness is avoided because they disappear during intercourse. They have no odour. Foams are also applied with an applicator and come out of containers resembling the foams men use in shaving. A chemical provides the means of contraception. While it is claimed that foams can be inserted several hours before intercourse, it is probably best that the interval be no longer than an hour. Foams are not expensive and can be bought at chemists with no prescription. As contraceptives, they can be rated as 'excellent'.

The most recent contraceptive device is the intra-uterine coil, a small plastic device which comes in different shapes and is designed to be inserted into the uterus by a doctor. It is left inside for months or even years. It is nearly as effective as the pill, but is not practicable for young girls because it is only appropriate for use by women who have had a child.

For those whose religion forbids them to use mechanical

or chemical devices, reliance is placed on what Catholics call the 'rhythm method'. The theory is that pregnancy is avoided by not having intercourse during the time the egg is coming out of the ovary, and descending the Fallopian tubes. It would be an excellent contraceptive method if one could be sure when this process was happening. But even if a girl kept an accurate record of her menstrual periods and knew exactly when the process began, fourteen days before the next menstruation, and refrained from intercourse during the few hours of the month when ovulation was taking place, it would still be safe only if she had exactly regular periods. Many girls do not. Moreover, she would have to ovulate only once a month. Some girls do it more often than that. It is easy to see, then, why this method is so uncertain and unsafe. I would not recommend it before marriage.

Another non-mechanical method of contraception is withdrawal, commonly practised by young people, in which the penis is withdrawn from the vagina just before ejaculation takes place. It sounds simple and easy, but it is neither. For one thing, it is done at the height of sexual excitement, when both people are most involved with the act and neither wants to stop; consequently it is not very enjoyable. Sometimes the excitement is so great that the boy will not be able to stop at all. Even if he does so, however, it may not be quite soon enough; ejaculation may have begun sooner than he thinks. Besides, there may be enough sperm in the lubricating fluid from the penis before ejaculation to make a girl pregnant. Clearly, withdrawal is not only unsatisfactory but unsafe as well.

Sometimes a girl thinks she is practising contraception by washing out her vagina after intercourse with an antiseptic in water (see Chapter 11). It requires apparatus a young girl is not likely to carry around, and in any case it is a poor and ineffective method of contraception, pregnancy often resulting anyway. Some antiseptics also burn or irritate the vagina.

Except for the pill, no matter what method is used, there is one drawback in the very idea of contraception. Girls, as I have said, generally have a more romantic concept of sex and intercourse than boys. Consequently many of them have no conscious intention of having intercourse but get carried away by the mood of the moment and the situation, and have it without any thought of contraception. Thus any planning about whether a boy has a condom on before intercourse runs against the natural inclination of the girl. For most of them, such planning ahead takes away a good part of the pleasure of intercourse. They want it to be spontaneous and uninterrupted mechanically. While I understand this feeling, I can only say that the surest way to get pregnant is to be overcome by romance and the pleasure of the moment without regard for the outcome and without doing something about the possible consequences.

Let us assume that contraceptives were not used, then, or bad ones were used and a girl becomes pregnant. She has four options open to her. She can get married, but usually this is a poor choice because both boy and girl are likely to be too young to start family life. Few boys can support a girl at that age, and, for both of them, it means that schooling will be interrupted or even ended. As I have noted before, marriages that begin under these circumstances are usually not so successful as those not made as the result of necessity.

The second option is to have the baby without marrying the boy. Again, this is not often a good choice because the girl is unable to support the baby herself and give it the proper environment. She must also face the disapproval of society, directed against both the child and herself.

A third option is to have the baby but have it adopted

immediately. There are numerous complications here. The girl will have to be able to leave her home and neighbourhood for five or six months, for one thing. For another, many girls who go through the nine months of pregnancy and birth don't want to give up their baby, no matter how sensible it may be to do so. Putting one's baby out for adoption is a painful process at best.

The fourth option is abortion. In some countries abortion is available virtually on demand. In Britain this is not quite the case, though most of the difficulties in the way of obtaining an abortion, and most of the unhappiness and danger too, were removed by the Abortion Act of 1967.

This Act came into force in April 1968 and from then until the end of January 1969 over 23,000 legal abortions were carried out in England and Wales. One of the Act's main purposes was to do away with the need for illegal 'back-street' abortionists who, medically qualified or not (and usually not), would perform the operation discreetly but often for exorbitant fees, and equally often in extremely unhygienic and dangerous conditions. Also the Act made it unnecessary for any girl to try to bring on an abortion herself, by taking special potions or 'women's pills' or, worse, pushing some sharp instrument into her vagina.

Done carelessly, or by someone who does not know what she is doing, terminating a pregnancy is an extremely risky business. It can leave a girl permanently unable to have children and it can even be fatal. Most doctors have seen during their professional lives some of the tragic results of bungled abortions and the best that can be said for the illegal abortionists was that they fulfilled a social need.

If the operation is performed in proper conditions by qualified people, the risk is small. There is still some slight danger, as there is with any surgical operation. Just how great that danger is can be judged from the fact that in the first eight months of the Abortion Act, three women died out of the 23,641 who had the operation.

As a rule the operation itself is not, by modern standards, very complicated or difficult. In most cases a girl who goes to hospital to have it done can be home again within two or three days. Some private nursing homes allow patients to go in and have the operation and go home the same day, but this is seldom done in NHS hospitals.

A doctor may use one of a number of techniques when he terminates a pregnancy. The most usual is to dilate, or open out, the neck of the womb in order to scoop out the embryo inside. Another method, which is becoming more widely used, involves using a suction apparatus which rapidly empties the womb of its contents: this method is called 'vacuum aspiration'. Still another method, usually done only if the pregnancy is well advanced, is to remove the growing baby by cutting into the patient's abdomen and into her womb.

Under the 1967 Act it is legal for a doctor to terminate a pregnancy provided certain conditions are met.

The conditions are these. The operation has to be performed by a registered medical practitioner and, except for emergencies, must be done in a National Health Service hospital, or in some place which has been approved by the Department of Health. (In 1970, 46 nursing homes were given this official approval, the majority of them in the southern counties of England.)

Furthermore, two doctors have to certify that an abortion is in their opinion necessary on one or other of the following grounds. First, if going on with the pregnancy were to involve a risk to the pregnant woman's mental or physical health or to her life – a risk greater than that of the operation itself. Secondly, if going on with the pregnancy were to threaten the physical or mental health of any children she already had – and again, the doctors would have to be of the opinion that the risk was greater than that of the operation. Thirdly, the operation would be allowable if there were a substantial danger of the child being born with some serious abnormality.

In an emergency, a doctor can act on his own, without another doctor's confirmation, to save a pregnant woman's life or to prevent some grave and lasting injury to her health. And in all cases, the doctor can take into account what the Act calls her 'actual or reasonably foreseeable environment'.

So in other words the provisions of the Abortion Act are wide-reaching and can be interpreted fairly generously. But on the other hand many doctors, and not only Roman Catholics, dislike terminating a pregnancy. Some object on religious, some on moral grounds. If they feel strongly enough, they are entitled to refuse to have anything to do with an abortion, and nurses can do the same. But a doctor who feels this way is expected to refer a girl, if she asks, to some other doctor who would be prepared to make the necessary arrangements. If he will not do this, there are several organizations which will put girls in touch with doctors who are sympathetic to the provisions of the 1967 Act. A good source of advice on these organizations, and on the whole problem, is the local family planning clinic.

Bearing all these conditions in mind, having an abortion under the National Health Service is like having any other hospital operation. The first step is to go to one's own family doctor. Medical ethics demand, by the way, that anything a girl tells him should be confidential. If he agrees that the operation should be done, he will make the necessary arrangements and probably refer the girl to a hospital where the operation can be performed. One possible difficulty is that the lack of hospital beds may mean having to wait for a vacancy. And it is not unknown for a patient to have to wait so long that the operation becomes a much more serious matter than it would have been early in the pregnancy. This is one reason why some girls prefer to go to a private nursing home, where they will, of course, have to pay. The charge varies between £100 and £200 and may be even higher. Generally a girl who went to a private clinic or nursing home would first consult a general practitioner, or family doctor. But some private establishments are prepared to accept a patient without insisting on a doctor's letter.

If a girl thinks she is pregnant, the first thing she should do is to make certain she is. This is done by means of a medical test, using a sample of urine. The laboratory test costs about £2, and it can be done through a doctor or a Pregnancy Testing Clinic.

Once pregnancy is established, the best advice that can be given is to do what I am sure most girls most dread. Nevertheless, it is her parents she should turn to first for help. I am ready to admit that there are a good many parents who give their daughters a rough time and in general treat her shabbily if she becomes pregnant before marriage, but, on the other hand, there are many others who prove to be warm, loving and protective in this situation. Naturally, they will probably blame the boy and be angry with him, but that is only to be expected. Sometimes there are other adults in the community a girl can turn to, like the family doctor or minister, or often an adult in the family she feels especially close to, possibly an aunt or an uncle or an older, married sister.

If abortion is the option decided upon, remember that it must be done before the end of the third month because the foetus is large enough after that to make the operation dangerous. No competent abortionist will operate after that date.

One thing to be avoided absolutely is reliance on self-administered drugs or some other means to bring on a miscarriage, which loosens the foetus from the uterine walls and lets it slip down into the vagina and out of the body. The drugs popularly believed to cause miscarriage – quinine, castor oil, ergot, among others – almost never do. If they do, it is only in cases where the girl would have had the miscarriage in any case. About one in twenty pregnancies ends in miscarriage in the ordinary course of events. However, if a girl is afraid she might have become pregnant, she can get pills (or an injection) from her doctor if she sees him immediately (no later than the third day after intercourse). This medication is often effective in stopping pregnancy.

Even worse is to try to induce abortion by some means like falling on the stomach, inserting something into the uterus or jumping from a high place to jar the foetus loose. These are extremely dangerous practices. They lead often to injury, infection or death, and even if they were likely to work, the danger would be far too great.

Pregnancy, however, is not the only possible consequence of intercourse. Venereal diseases are transmitted only by some sort of sexual contact, and that danger is present, too. Gonorrhoea and syphilis are the two most common kinds of venereal disease. The symptoms are the same for girls as for boys, by and large, but because the girl's sex organs are more hidden, they will be more difficult to spot. In gonorrhoea, for example, a boy notices a burning in his penis when he urinates, appearing eight to fifteen days after he is infected. A little later, pus with a characteristic and rather unpleasant odour begins to drip from the penis. Girls, on the other hand, will have a painful irritation in the lining of the urethra and it, too, produces pus, but since the secretion is not so easily noticed as in boys, a girl may think she has nothing more than a vaginal infection.

In syphilis, a more serious matter, the germ invades the body through any mucous membrane; in the girl this can be the vagina or the mouth. The first symptom is a single sore, not painful, followed by a rash which may appear on any part of the body. It is a light rash, lasting for only a short time, and so may be unnoticed. The sore appears most often on the penis of the boy or in the vagina of the girl. It appears about sixty days after the infection and goes away in time. If the disease is not treated, however, it continues to fester in the body silently, although it may seem to disappear entirely and not return for months or even years. But when it does return, it will be in a much more violent state, able to do serious damage to body organs and eventually, if unchecked, may even result in death.

A girl develops the same characteristic syphilitic sore, or chancre, as the boy, but it may be hidden in the vagina or the mouth so that she may not know she has it. There is, incidentally, no truth to the common superstition that one can tell if a girl has venereal disease by pouring whisky or Coke on her sex organ, and if it burns, she is infected. The only way a girl can tell is if she has a visible chancre on the lips of her vagina or has a discharge of pus from the urethra.

Venereal disease is not the terrible scourge it was. Once it was possible to cure gonorrhoea only by a long and often painful treatment, which was not always effective. Syphilis was known as 'the great killer' for centuries and ran rampant in the world. It was the discovery of penicillin and the sulpha drugs that turned the tide. Today, for gonorrhoea, the medication is a shot of penicillin, which clears it up with one to three shots in ninety-five per cent of the cases. If penicillin fails, sulpha drugs are employed. Shots of penicillin are also used to treat syphilis. The series lasts about five days and is almost always effective.

A girl who has any symptoms of venereal disease, or thinks she has, should consult the doctor. Young girls and

boys are likely to be afraid that he will tell their parents if
they do have venereal disease, but most doctors respect
the confidential nature of the relationship between doctor
and patient, even if it is a family doctor who may have
delivered his patient. Nevertheless, the doctor is required
by law to report the case to the local health authorities,
although not all do so. Unquestionably there are a great
many unreported cases. The health authorities are interested
in only one thing. They want to know where the girl or
boy got the disease, and they have the authority to ask
them whom they have been having intercourse with and
will examine these persons to see where the infection
originated. If you don't want to talk to your family doctor,
the easiest place to have a check-up is a special VD clinic.
These special clinics are held at most big hospitals. Advice
and treatment are completely private and confidential. You
can go without a letter from your GP and all treatment is
free. You can either go straight to the hospital and ask
where the clinic is, or telephone the hospital and ask to
speak to the receptionist at the clinic. Many people who
go to these clinics because they are worried that they have
caught VD turn out not to have it at all. So either way, you
can't lose from a check-up. If you have VD, you will be on
the way to a cure; if you haven't, your fears will be put
at rest.

Whatever the consequences of intercourse may be, and
I have covered the important ones here, the very best advice I can give any girl is to learn about these consequences
before she makes any decisions about intercourse. If she
possesses the knowledge beforehand, she will not only be
far better able to make a decision, but the consequences, if
they come, will not be unexpected. Beyond that, the most
difficult consequences of intercourse to handle for most
girls are the feelings of fear or guilt, or both, the act may

inspire. Since these factors are the enemy of any meaningful human relationship, a girl who finds that she cannot handle these feelings would be better off not to have intercourse at all, and thus avoid the struggle over consequences entirely.

But even if there is no fear or guilt, and even if a girl has weighed her decision carefully before taking so important a step (and, unfortunately, that is not very common), intercourse may produce unforeseen psychological consequences. A girl may feel that, after all, she is not ready for such a relationship or that she has created a situation which disturbs and upsets the way she wants to live. Sometimes, in a moment of regret, she may feel that she has given herself away too cheaply for no more than a quick sensation. It is not uncommon, too, for her to see her partner in a different light and to be disappointed in him as a human being.

Obviously, as all these consequences indicate, intercourse is not a matter to be taken lightly or casually. It demands much more than a physical response. The girl who thinks before she leaps has the advantage.

9
Masturbation

MASTURBATION has been defined in several ways, but the one I prefer calls it: 'A deliberate self-stimulation which results in sexual arousal.' There are those, however, who think of self-masturbation in a much broader way. They regard it as any kind of self-stimulation which gives pleasure, a definition broad enough to include rubbing the nose and riding on a roller coaster.

Our attitudes about masturbation stem from the Judaeo-Christian religious tradition. The founders of these faiths believed that sex must be only for the purpose of procreation, and because masturbation does not result in pregnancy, organized religions have always been solidly against it. Today these attitudes are gradually changing. Even the churches, or at least some of them, now look upon sex as something pleasurable in its own right, an act not necessarily leading to procreation. But taboos which have existed for centuries are not so easily changed, and there are still a great many adults, including probably most parents, who are against masturbation, even though they might not be able to say exactly why. Their opposition has been reinforced by the teachings of Freud and his followers, which say, in effect, that masturbation may be all right for young children, when it is a part of growing up, but that it is childish, immature and undesirable for older people.

It is not surprising, then, that a large number of girls are influenced by these negative attitudes and, when they masturbate, find that they feel guilty about it. This is unfortunate because, if girls allow the ancient social taboos to interfere, they will detract substantially from the pleasure they are capable of getting out of it. Masturbation is only a part of ordinary sexual activity, like petting or intercourse, and there is no more reason to feel guilty about it than about anything else we do sexually as human beings.

It can be said against masturbation that if a girl's moral philosophy or her religion tells her that sex is only for procreation and therefore it is morally wrong to masturbate, all the arguments for masturbation will have no meaning for her. There are girls, too, who feel that if parents and other respected adults are against it, they must conform to their attitudes. I believe in respecting these feelings, and I am convinced that girls who do masturbate in spite of such strong moral feelings against it will find that it does them more harm than good in a psychological sense.

It has been argued that masturbation is harmful because it fixates a girl at that level and makes it difficult or impossible for her to enjoy intercourse. As indicated earlier, there is no truth in this argument. In fact, studies show that girls who learn to have orgasm through masturbation have an easier time in responding to intercourse than those who do not. It is also asserted that masturbation does all kinds of physical harm to young girls. If we believed this argument, we would have to accept the notion that facial spots, poor posture, dullness of mind, cancer, stomach upsets, sterility, headaches and kidney trouble, among other ills, are the result of masturbation. All these troubles and many others have been laid at its door, but there is absolutely no medical evidence that there is any relationship between masturbation and illness of any kind. The only harm known to come from masturbating is an occasional local irritation caused by a great deal of friction or an occasional minor infection caused by the insertion of some unclean object into the vagina or the urethra.

On the other hand, there are several reasons why

masturbation is beneficial. First, it can bring a great deal of pleasure to a girl, especially if she masturbates to the point of orgasm. It is pleasurable without orgasm, too, but stopping short may leave her momentarily frustrated and uneasy, with a good deal of congestion in her genitals.

As I have mentioned earlier, masturbation also can teach a girl how to have orgasm, and it does so in the most simple, direct way possible, so that it will be easier for her to have orgasm when she does have intercourse. And there are other reasons in favour of this activity. Because no one else is involved, masturbation is easily available as long as there is privacy. It also permits a girl to learn how her own body reacts and allows her to experiment with herself so that she can more easily teach someone else the things that make her feel good sexually. Then there are other, though minor, things on the plus side : the fact that there is no danger of venereal disease or of pregnancy; that it does no harm to her or anyone else; that it offers a variety of sexual experience and provides a way of developing one's fantasy life.

The contrast between boys and girls practising masturbation is a sharp one. By the age of fifteen, about twenty-five per cent of girls have masturbated to the point of orgasm, while the figure would be virtually a hundred per cent for boys. Eventually more than sixty per cent of women masturbate, but much of it occurs in their later years, even in marriage. For the young girls who do masturbate, the average frequency is about once every two or three weeks, although there is a great deal of variation. Some do it many times a week, others only very infrequently.

Most boys learn how to masturbate by hearing about it from other boys, while most girls discover it for themselves. Again, this reflects the fact that boys do much more talking about sex among themselves than girls do. As many as a quarter of the girls who do not begin masturbating until they are in their early twenties or older still discover it by themselves. Oddly enough, some girls masturbate for a long time before they realize that this is what they are doing.

Girls also learn about the practice from books like this one, or from other girls or boys, who tell them about it. Less than half the girls learn about it this way, but that is how three fourths of the boys find out. About one girl in every ten learns of masturbation as the result of petting, and about the same number through seeing someone else do it. Only about three per cent of girls learn through a homosexual experience; the figure is much higher for boys. Another surprise in this era of sexual freedom is to discover that there are so many girls who have never known it was possible to masturbate.

However it is learned, the techniques are the same. As I noted in Chapter 2, the clitoris in the female is like the penis of the male, so it is not surprising that most girls masturbate by rubbing it or the part of the vulva immediately around it. In this technique, the girl usually moves a finger or several fingers or perhaps her whole hand gently and rhythmically over this section, sometimes applying steady and increased pressure as she builds towards orgasm. She may also use the heel of her foot or some other object placed against this area. Some girls discover that a very gentle pressure is all that is required, while others need to apply so much pressure that it takes one hand on top of another to accomplish it. This way of masturbating is usually done while the girl is lying on her back or perhaps sitting up, but it is also done while lying on the stomach, with one hand underneath placed over the vulva and a finger manipulating the clitoris.

About ten per cent of girls who masturbate do so by crossing their legs and in this way exert steady and rhythmic pressure on the whole genital area. A smaller number learn by developing muscular tension through their bodies. One way to accomplish this is to lie face down with buttocks moving rhythmically forward and against each other. In this position, a girl may press some part of her organ against the bed or the pillow. However, it is not the stimulation of something against the sex organ that brings her to orgasm, but rather the muscular tension in the body, resembling the tensions developed in the motions of intercourse. Other ways of building up muscular tension include climbing up a pole or a rope or even chinning on parallel bars. About fifty per cent of women find that their breasts are erotically sensitive, and one girl in ten will stimulate her breast with one hand while she rubs her clitoris with the other. Few girls, however, can achieve orgasm by breast stimulation alone.

Although about twenty per cent insert something in their vaginas to masturbate, few of them do this regularly. The most common object inserted is a finger. When this is done, a girl pulls her hand up against the top of the organ so that the clitoris and the *labia minora* are stimulated at the same time. There are a few girls who get more satisfaction out of deep vaginal penetration than they do from stimulating the clitoris, but the number is small. Boys believe the insertion of something is always the way girls masturbate. They think in terms of the penis being inserted into the vagina and find it difficult to realize that the girl's area of erotic stimulation is the clitoris, not the vagina.

There are a variety of other techniques, used by a limited number of girls, such as rubbing the organ against a table corner or some other object, letting streams of water run against the clitoris, using vibrators against the clitoris, and by inserting objects into the urethra or the anus. About two per cent of girls are able to have orgasm by means of conscious fantasy alone. Only one boy in a thousand is able to do this.

If there is no attempt to delay the speed of orgasm, the average girl has a climax in less than four minutes, although some can do it in only a few seconds. Because in intercourse the male usually has some trouble in holding back his orgasm until the girl is ready, it is advisable for boys to learn to delay it. This can be practised in masturbation. For the same reason, it is good for girls not to delay it when they masturbate, even though they may find that they can go on and on and have two or more orgasms in succession.

When boys begin to masturbate, about the time they enter puberty, they tend to continue the experience regularly until some other kind of sexual activity begins. Even after they start to pet and have intercourse, they continue to masturbate with regularity, but with decreasing frequency. Girls, on the other hand, tend to be much less regular about their masturbation. They may do it a great deal for a period of time, perhaps as often as twenty times a week, or once a day for two months – and then they will suddenly stop for a longer period of time. Stopping may be the result of guilt feelings, but often it is simply lack of interest. For quite a few girls there seems to be an absence of sexual desire, a lack of pressure being built up because of limited sexual activity until it must explode in orgasm, as is the case with boys. Girls find it hard to understand that boys have this pressure, which is frequently with them, just as it sometimes seems incomprehensible to boys that girls can take sex or leave it alone so easily.

Another difference between the sexes lies in what girls think about while they masturbate. About a third of them don't appear to think about anything except the sensation itself. Girls who do fantasize usually think only of the experiences they have already had. For example, a girl who has only kissed with a boy and has gone no further will usually fantasize kissing a boy when she masturbates, while a boy who has only kissed will probably think of intercourse. Girls also tend to fantasize more general things, like being married or lying down with a boy or being in some beautiful, romantic setting. Boys are much more specific. They develop scenarios and almost always the genitals are involved in their fantasies.

Girls who do have specific sexual fantasies sometimes find them disturbing. They may think of intercourse with teachers, with their fathers or brothers, or they may imagine that they are prostitutes or are being raped.

Let me add that the only harm that can come from such fantasies is a feeling of guilt. Sex fantasies, like other daydreams, are part of normal life and should be regarded as such. Boys have these fantasies, too. They imagine having sex with teachers, or their sisters, or their mothers or fathers, and sometimes they even imagine an orgy with several girls and boys or perhaps just boys. They may think of having sex with a particular girl or boy, or a grown man or woman, or forcing someone else to have sex with them, or of being forced themselves. Obviously, they have a more elaborate fantasy life than girls, which is only natural because they are more preoccupied with sex. In either sex, the chances are astronomical that any of these masturbation fantasies will ever come true, but they add to the excitement. When a girl or boy stops fantasizing and comes back to the real world, real things are dealt with in a realistic way and no harm is done.

Both girls and boys sometimes masturbate because of a conflict in their lives which is not sexual. Boredom, frustration and loneliness are motivations. Sometimes they do it because they have a poor opinion of themselves, don't know how to get along with the other sex, or find themselves in constant conflict with parents. If they are under great pressure at school, boys particularly tend to masturbate more. Masturbation does relieve the tension, whatever it is, temporarily, but if it seems that the primary motive for masturbation is for any of these nonsexual reasons, youngsters ought to get some counselling help and try to solve their problems.

The only other source of sexual feeling I have not mentioned is the activity that results from sexual dreams. This is far more prevalent among boys than girls. Few teenage girls have orgasms when they are asleep, although it is fairly common in older women, nearly half of whom do. For teenagers, however, the percentage is small. The sexual dreams girls have are about the same as the fantasies they have when they masturbate, and there are the same differences in the content of the girls' and the boys' dreams as occur in fantasy.

In our complicated society, girls (as well as boys) should understand that there are many different attitudes to masturbation, as I indicated at the beginning of the chapter. Some think it sinful and harmful to health – the view of traditional people and often of parents. Those with strong religious beliefs think it distracts people from the true purpose of sexuality, which they conceive of as marriage and reproduction. Then there are those who regard themselves as neutral on the subject, saying that it needs further study and meanwhile they don't intend to encourage it as something positively good. Finally, there are those who take the liberal view ('permissive', in the eyes of those cited above), who believe that masturbation is not only harmless but positively good and healthy, and ought to be encouraged because it helps young people to grow up sexually in a natural way. That is my belief, as I think any girl who reads this book will understand.

Everyone who is growing up, however, has to learn what is acceptable public behaviour and what is acceptable only in private. But because something is private doesn't mean it is bad, or inferior, or dirty. Masturbating in private is an acceptable way of releasing sexual tension and an important part of growing up. The only enemies are fear, anxiety and guilt, and they must be understood, dealt with and eliminated.

10

Homosexuality

HOMOSEXUAL behaviour is sexual behaviour between two people of the same sex. To understand it better, one should remember that for behaviour to be sexual it must involve more than just physical contact and must result in some change in the body – deeper breathing, a warm skin, a rapid pulse or some other symptom that can be identified as sexual. By this measurement, two girls walking arm in arm, or with their arms around each other, or kissing, are not necessarily engaged in homosexual behaviour, although they could be if they have sexual feelings for each other when they are doing it.

To define homosexual behaviour more exactly, a woman who has sexual relations with another woman or who is aroused sexually by another woman is called a 'lesbian'. The word comes from the Greek island of Lesbos, where in ancient times the poet Sappho lived and wrote of the joys of lesbian love in glowing verse which has become part of classic literature.

One thing that confuses a great many people is thinking of homosexuality as something separate and distinct from heterosexuality, which means sexual relations or attraction between members of the opposite sex. Because a girl is sexually aroused by or has relations with another girl doesn't mean she cannot have relations with boys, just as a girl who likes ice cream may also like pie. A girl may be exclusively heterosexual, meaning she has never had any sexual contact with another girl or been aroused by one. Or she can be exclusively homosexual. There are probably two to three per cent of girls who fall in the latter category. About a quarter fall between the two extremes; these girls have some combination of heterosexual and homosexual behaviour in their lives.

A common occurrence in growing up is for a girl to become very fond of another girl and have warm, affectionate feelings towards her. We call it a 'crush', an old-fashioned word for which there doesn't seem to be any modern substitute. Sometimes it is hard to draw the line between a crush and a sexual feeling. For example, I'm thinking of fourteen-year-old Jane, who is constantly in the company of her girl-friend Betty. They spend hours together, talking about their experiences, their plans for the future, other girls, school and the thousand things all girls find to talk about. They often put their arms around each other, and, when they are separated during the summer vacation, they think about each other and write letters. They always feel especially good in each other's company. This is a typical picture of a schoolgirl crush, of the kind millions of girls have known. It is something almost all girls have experienced in one degree or another.

Up to this point, there is nothing homosexual in their behaviour. But suppose that one night, while Jane is sleeping at Betty's house, they embrace each other in their customary warm, affectionate way and something happens that hasn't happened before. Sexual feelings are aroused. They begin to stroke each other's bodies, especially the breasts and sex organ, and experience sexual excitement from the contact. They may or may not have an orgasm as a result. It is at this point that the crush turns into a homosexual response.

Many girls have had such experiences and have not become lesbians. Their response to each other was no more than a sexual extension of their past relationship, and perhaps it never happened again or was repeated only infrequently. But if they had become so absorbed in their sexual relationship with each other that they excluded any physical contact with boys or displayed no interest in them, then they would have been well on the way to becoming lesbians. It is the *amount* of homosexual contact in relation to the amount of heterosexual involvement that appears to be the determining factor, not whether or not there is homosexual contact at all.

It seems to me the important thing is not whether a girl is in actual sexual contact with another girl, but what her relationship is with boys. If she restrains from having anything to do with them because of feelings of hostility, or because she is afraid of them, or because she wants to avoid going out and the problems it brings, then the development of her homosexual life will be taking place for negative reasons, rather than the positive one of enjoying a relationship with a girl on its own merits.

Often parents who restrict a girl from going out with boys, or put strict curbs on her behaviour with them, push a girl into exclusively female relationships which may turn out to be homosexual. Why shouldn't we permit this to happen, if that is what the girl wants to do? In this sense, there is nothing against it, but a girl may not understand that, by taking this sexual path, she is sentencing herself to live in the shadow of society's disapproval and is closing the door to marriage and children. Perhaps even worse, she is choosing this direction, or being forced into it, for the wrong reason, namely, because of a rejection of males rather than an acceptance of females.

Few people are able to accept the truth about themselves, which is that everyone is *potentially* capable of doing every act imaginable, including having homosexual relations, given the proper circumstances, conditioning and background. Everyone has latent homosexual tendencies in one degree or another, but it doesn't mean we will ever actually do anything about it or even be aware of it.

It is a common experience to be stirred by a sexual feeling towards someone of the same sex, through a fantasy, a dream or in some other way. This idea horrifies most people. If they have such a conscious thought, they feel intensely guilty about their 'perverted' feelings. Yet most people will never take part in a homosexual act, and their momentary thoughts or feelings will never interfere with their heterosexual lives. Once more, it is only guilt and fear that will plague them, if they permit it.

Nevertheless, girls are curious about lesbianism when they hear of it. They are at once repelled and fascinated. Often they ask, 'But what do they *do*?' It may surprise them to know that they do what girls and boys do together, except that they cannot have intercourse, since no penis is involved. Sometimes the sexual contact is no more than kissing, or tongue-kissing, but it may also go on to and include stroking the body and breasts, mutual masturbation, mouths on each other's sex organs, or lying together with sex organs against each other and going through the movements of intercourse.

Only about one girl in ten ever has specific homosexual contacts; nearly twice that number are aroused psychologically in a specific sexual way by other girls. For the girls who have actual contact, the average experience is about once in five weeks. Usually the experiences occur in clusters rather than spread out evenly, much like the incidence of masturbation.

There are no laws against lesbianism in Britain and there is more toleration for female homosexuals in Western society than for males.

Primarily this is because of our social inheritance from our Judaeo-Christian ancestors, who regarded women as little more than property, and so female sexual behaviour which did not affect males was of little concern to the lawmakers. Masturbation and homosexuality were virtually ignored among women, but they were offences punishable by death among men. Again, homosexuality was early identified with anal intercourse, so female homosexuality was not considered wrong. In our own time, people are not so much aware of lesbian behaviour in public as they are of the more obvious kind of homosexual behaviour among men. Then, too, people do not easily visualize homosexual behaviour between women, while they have a very clear idea (or think they do) of what happens between men. There are other reasons, but these are the chief ones which account for our surprising tolerance, when we are so intolerant of other kinds of sexual behaviour that are not 'normal'.

The attitudes of girls in general towards homosexual behaviour among their own sex is far less tolerant. One of the reasons girls are so concerned about their reputations is because they are so quick to condemn or reject other girls who do not do things the way they do or as the group does. The girl who wears a different kind of clothing or acts in a different way is often ostracized and rejected by the others. They must all conform to the fads and customs of the time or they are ridiculed. This is especially true of girls who display any homosexual behaviour. Ironically, it is their rejection by the rest of the group which is among the primary reasons they develop patterns of exclusive homosexuality, since they are then denied the possibility of heterosexuality.

One of the reasons we reject other people is fear of them or of what they might do; another is ignorance of their behaviour. One of the things I hope this book will accomplish is to provide more information about homosexuality so that some of the fear and ignorance leading to the rejection of other people will be diminished a little. I believe people should be accepted or rejected on the basis of themselves as individuals, rather than whether they like ice cream or pie.

There are a few lesbians who develop mannish mannerisms, both in the way they dress and in their actions, but only about five per cent of girls with active homosexual lives develop these characteristics. There are some girls so like boys we call them 'tomboys', but they usually have no homosexual inclinations at all. In the great majority of cases, it is impossible for a girl to tell whether or not her friends or acquaintances are engaged in homosexual behaviour. About fifteen per cent of boys are obviously homosexual, which means a girl will not be able, in most cases, to tell among the boys she knows which ones are involved in homosexual behaviour.

Another common misconception is that in a lesbian relationship one partner exclusively plays the male role and is called a 'butch', while the other exclusively plays the 'femme'. Although this does occur, in the great majority of cases, both partners play both roles.

There are occasions when a girl is seeing a boy and suspects he is having homosexual activity. Sometimes girls are so repulsed by the idea that they reject the boy, and this, of course, pushes him even farther in the direction of homosexuality. My feeling is that, if a girl accepts the boy as he is without making an issue of his homosexuality or becoming a rival, there may still be a good possibility that she will be able to work out a satisfactory relationship with him and that his homosexuality will fall into proper perspective in his life. If I may go back to my familiar analogy – just as one doesn't learn to like ice cream by giving up pie, so one doesn't learn to like heterosexuality by giving up homosexuality. This applies to girls as well as boys.

As I have noted, there are girls who like to dress in a mannish way, like boys, and a few carry it to such an extreme that they actually dress completely as males and think they *are* males. In rare cases, they even have operations to remove their breasts and have penises sewn to their bodies so they can perform as males. Most girls will probably never meet such a person. More common are males who want to become females; there are nearly a thousand cases in the United States of men who have been operated on successfully to accomplish this transformation.

Girls are sometimes faced with having a crush on an older woman, especially a teacher. It can be very flattering to have an older person take a personal interest in one, and most girls have had this experience in one degree or another. These relationships are often happy and helpful ones to a girl growing up, and they rarely lead to any sexual activity, as some adults fear. When sex does become the aim of the older woman's advances, whether or not she is a teacher, the situation is quite different from when an older man makes a sexual approach (see Chapter 5). An older woman's approach will be much more gradual and gentle. It is usually easier for a girl to say 'no' to an older woman than to put off the older man. If she is confronted with this problem, the girl should ask herself the same question as she did about the man : Why does this older person want to be involved with a young girl?

In conclusion, homosexual relationships can be as pleasurable, as deep and as worthwhile as relationships with males, but because our society is so oriented in the direction of heterosexuality and has such strong taboos against homosexuality, it seems to me that girls should think long and hard before rejecting sexual activity with boys in preference to girls.

11

Questions and Answers

IF there are questions girls want to ask about sex which have not been answered in the preceding pages, I hope they will find them here. These are questions which have actually been asked by several different groups of young girls. Readers may not find their own special questions, because obviously it would be impossible to set down the hundreds which might be asked. I urge readers who still have questions to seek the answers from a competent authority. To know is better than to wonder and imagine.

1. *Do boys have a different interest in sex from girls and a different ability to perform sexually?*

I have answered the first part of this question to some extent, but I can add that there are boys who, like girls, are 'late bloomers' in the sense that they are not interested in sex until their late teens, then have an active sex life. I had one patient, twenty-four years old, who had never had an erection in his life because he was low in male-hormone production. But then there are boys who seem to be interested in sex almost from the time they are born. They learn quickly to masturbate to orgasm and may do so several times a day. Sometimes they continue an active sexual life until they are old men. Most boys fall between these extremes. With both boys and girls, if an individual is a highly sexed person, there is not much that can be done to decrease it, and conversely, if one is on the low end of the scale, not much can be done to increase sexual activity to any appreciable extent. A girl (or boy) should accept her (his) sexuality, whatever it is, no matter where she (he) falls on the scale.

2. *How long can sperm live?*

They can live in the vagina from one to two days. Some have even been kept alive, under special conditions, for eight days or more. When sperm are not in a warm, moist, alkaline place, they die quickly.

3. *What is circumcision?*

Girls are often curious about this, especially if they have had a chance to see the different appearance of a penis when this operation has been performed. There is a loose piece of skin extending to the end or beyond the end of the penis. This is called the 'foreskin'. It may be cut off by a doctor a few days after a baby is born. This procedure is known as 'circumcision'. In England, unlike America, it is not carried out as a matter of course, and is relatively unusual. The advantage of circumcision is that it makes it easier to keep the head of the penis and the part just beyond it cleaner, although actually there is nothing unclean about an uncircumcised man's penis.

The Jewish faith requires that the male be circumcised, and the operation itself is a religious ritual. There are other reasons, too, for circumcision. Sometimes the foreskin sticks to the head of the penis (this is called 'adhesion') and circumcision is required to get it unstuck. In other cases, the foreskin has such a small opening that the head of the penis cannot be pushed through. This condition is called 'phimosis'. Sometimes it is possible in such cases to stretch the foreskin without circumcision. Boys also have to contend with a white, cheese-like substance forming behind the head of the penis, called 'smegma'. It has to be washed away every day because it has an unpleasant odour.

4. *What is 'stone ache', or 'lover's balls'?*

In the chapter on orgasm, I explained that girls may get an ache in their groin because they have petted heavily or masturbated but not to the point of orgasm, when sexual tension is relieved. This also happens to boys. They, too, get aches in the groin when they have been petting for a long time with erection but without orgasm. Boys believe these aches to be in their testicles and call this condition by the slang term above. Its cause in both sexes is congestion, which leads to muscle contraction. It is the aching of these contracted muscles which is felt as pain.

5. What is impotence?

It is something girls don't have to worry about as far as their own anatomy is concerned, but it is a serious problem where their sexual partners are involved. The most common kind of impotence is erectile impotence, in which the male cannot get an erection. It may happen to a young boy when he is frightened, or if he is fearful he may not be able to get one. Less common is ejaculatory impotence, which happens when a male can get an erection but is unable to ejaculate. Impotence is usually caused by anxiety and disappears when the causes of the anxiety are removed.

6. What are other common words for the penis?

Girls are likely to hear at least some of the long list of synonyms for penis. Most commonly, they may hear it called a 'cock', 'dick', 'tool', 'pecker', or 'prick'.

7. What are other words for testicles?

Again, this will clear up some mysterious references girls hear in conversation or read in books. The two most common synonyms are 'balls' and 'bollocks', but there are many others.

8. What are other names for masturbation?

One or two are used in common by both sexes, like 'playing with yourself', but most of the others are words boys use, like 'jacking off', and 'jerking off' and 'beating your meat'. There are dozens of others.

9. What are other words for sexual intercourse?

Among the words acceptable in society are the two used

by doctors and those who write seriously about sex – 'coitus' and 'copulation'. The other synonyms – and there are literally hundreds of them, since this is one of the most common words in the English language – have not been accepted until recently, but now many of them appear in films, the theatre, in some newspapers and magazines, and all of them can be found in popular novels. A few of the more common words are 'fuck', 'screw', 'lay', 'sleep with', 'shag', 'bang', 'jazz'.

10. *What is the vagina?*

To repeat a little, the vagina is a tubelike structure, about three and a half inches in depth, extremely expandable. The penis enters it during intercourse. The whole structure of the female sex organ, including the vulva and the vagina, has many other names in common usage, just as the penis does. Among the most common are 'cunt' and 'pussy'.

11. *What is the clitoris?*

Again to repeat, in case anyone missed it earlier, the clitoris is a small, pealike structure at the top of the inner lips of the vulva but enfolded by the outer lips. It is the female equivalent of the male penis and is the focal point of stimulation in masturbation and petting.

12. *Are there times when a girl either doesn't want or can't have intercourse?*

The times when a girl *wants* intercourse vary greatly from girl to girl, but on the average, girls are more aroused for the day or two just before they menstruate, and a little less so again for the day or two following menstruation. A third likely time is during the menstrual period. This, however, is not true for every girl. There are those who do not vary that much in their sexual feeling. While there is no harm in having intercourse when a girl is menstruating, many don't want to have it then because they have cramps, because they think it is too messy or because of social taboos. This is especially true of those who follow the

Jewish religion, which considers it unclean and wrong. When they feel like having sex, girls are usually reacting more to the mood or the occasion. Quite naturally, if they have just had a quarrel with a boy, or they are feeling sulky or pouty about something, or if the time and place just doesn't seem right to them, they are not likely to want even to pet, much less to have intercourse. Occasionally, too, there are medical reasons why a girl should not have intercourse, particularly when she has an infection in her vagina or urethra.

13. *Do particular foods or drugs pep up the sex drive?*

The answer is no. If a girl wants to stimulate her sex drive (and not many would think of doing anything about it), she should get plenty of sleep, eat good, nourishing food and in general keep in good health. Among the old wives' tales about this subject is the superstition that foods like raw oysters, eggs or malted milk stimulate sexual performance. There is no truth in this idea. A girl should never permit a boy, nor permit herself, to use the powdered drug known as 'Spanish fly', or cantharides. It is commonly believed that the application of this drug will make the female extremely excited sexually, but what it actually does is to irritate the lining of the urethra, and if it is taken in sufficient quantity, it is highly poisonous. It has no effect on sexuality. For centuries people have looked for medicines or drugs to help stimulate them or their partners sexually. Nothing has ever been found that will do it except the injection of male hormones in men, and unfortunately this procedure may have dangerous side effects.

14. *What is a 'cherry'?*

This is the slang term for the hymen. The fact that it is erroneously believed hymens are never broken until penetrated by the male penis leads to such other slang phrases as 'picking a cherry' or 'getting a cherry'. By this is meant that a boy has had intercourse with a virgin, that is, a girl who has never had intercourse before and so, it is presumed incorrectly, must have an intact hymen.

15. *What is a whore?*

This very old name is applied to a girl or woman who has intercourse for money. The technical name is 'prostitute'. But again there are synonyms: 'tarts', 'streetwalkers', and 'call girls'.

16. *What is a pimp?*

A pimp is a man who manages a prostitute and takes a portion of her earnings. He is her business manager, occasionally getting customers for her, but usually not. In common usage, however, 'to pimp' means getting something illegally for someone else and is also sometimes used as a general term of contempt for a man who is weak, shifty or worthless.

17. *What is a male prostitute?*

A man who has sexual relations with another man for money. In male prostitution, the customer pays for the privilege of having the prostitute ejaculate, unlike with female prostitutes. There are also a few male prostitutes who are paid by women.

18. *What is a hermaphrodite?*

A true hermaphrodite is one who has the gonads (that is, testicles and ovaries) of both sexes. Few of these individuals exist, but there are pseudo-hermaphrodites, who are anatomically somewhere between the two sexes – a boy with a tiny penis, like a clitoris, perhaps; or a girl with a large clitoris, almost large enough to be a penis. Corrective surgery can often make these people more like a male or a female. Other pseudo-hermaphrodites may be a man who has large breasts like a woman's, or a woman with no breasts at all, or a woman with hair on her face, like a man – the 'bearded woman' of the circus and the carnival sideshow. These people are not really hermaphrodites. The trouble usually lies in a hormone imbalance. Boys often use corruptions of the word, like 'amorphadite' or 'morphadite' because they do not know the correct word, 'hermaphrodite'.

19. *What is castration?*

Once more, something girls need have no fear of, because it means cutting off the testicles. Since these are the main source of male hormones, an adolescent boy who has been castrated will have no growth of hair on his face, and the rest of his body hair will become fine and silky, while his voice remains high. He cannot ejaculate and often cannot get an erection. The word for such a person is 'eunuch' (pronounced yew-nuk). The older a man is, the less effect there will be if he is castrated.

20. *What are common names for gonorrhoea?*

Most often used are 'the clap' and 'the drips'.

21. *What are common names for syphilis?*

Most often used are 'the syph' and 'the pox', although there are several others.

22. *What is abnormal sex?*

I can't really answer this question because the word 'abnormal' is so ambiguous. Let me demonstrate what I mean. The word can mean something that is unusual or rare, so by that definition it would be abnormal to have intercourse by hanging from the chandelier because, I think it is safe to say, very few people have intercourse in this position. By that definition, however, masturbation would have to be considered normal because most boys masturbate. Homosexuality, too, would be almost normal because so many boys are involved in it.

Another way of defining 'abnormal' is to say that it is anything which is unnatural. Since human sexual behaviour is like that of other animals, it is natural. All mammals, of which humans are a species, engage in practically every kind of sex, including petting, masturbation and homosexuality, so by this definition there is essentially nothing humans do sexually that is abnormal.

A third way to look at 'abnormal' is through the eyes of society. We can look to both our laws and our churches for guidance here, although they are not always in complete agreement. For example, it is not against the law to masturbate, but some religions think it is wrong. On the other hand, it is against the law in the United States to put one's mouth on the sex organ of another person. Many religious leaders do not believe this is wrong, and most husbands and wives do it.

By and large, most of our sexual behaviour outside of marriage is considered wrong by the law, religion or both.

Still another way to look at 'abnormal' is to consider what sexual acts do harm to other people. Things like forcing other people to engage in sexual behaviour against their will, or to lie or cheat or seduce them into doing what they don't want to do would be considered abnormal.

It is easy to see, then, what a complicated business it is trying to decide what is abnormal sex, and that is why I suggest that the question cannot be answered.

23. *What is a wet dream?*

This is something that most often happens to boys, but can happen to girls as well, as I have remarked in the chapter on masturbation. For the boy, he wakes up some night or in the morning to discover that he has had an ejaculation while he was asleep. This may puzzle or frighten some boys who have heard that loss of semen in sleep is somehow damaging, which, of course, is not true. The 'wet dream' is simply the result of sexual excitement caused by dreaming which eventually reaches the usual climax with the emission of semen (for boys). It is not, as some think, an automatic substitute for intercourse or even a means of relieving sexual tension. In fact, it may often follow a sex experience.

24. *What is adultery, and what is fornication?*

Adultery is sexual experience when one or both persons are married but not to each other. Fornication is intercourse when neither partner is married.

25. *What would happen if a human being had intercourse with an animal?*

In spite of all the legends and fairy tales about it, no pregnancy will occur. In fact, about one out of five boys who live on farms or else visit one during summer holidays have intercourse, or attempt it, with animals. Only one or two of a hundred boys who live in cities ever practise such behaviour. Any of the farm animals may become a sexual object – ponies, calves, sheep, pigs, even chickens or ducks. Dogs are also used, but cats rarely. Intercourse with animals is usually infrequent among the boys who practise it, but some build up a strong emotional attachment to a particular animal and have intercourse with it on a regular basis. This behaviour is against the law and severe penalties can be provided for violation, not to mention the social ridicule which accompanies its discovery. Technically, intercourse with animals is known as 'bestiality'.

While there are cases of girls having sexual activity, or even intercourse, with animals, especially dogs, it is much more rare than among boys.

26. *Can humans and other animals mate and have young?*

They can mate, as indicated above, but they cannot become pregnant. Animals of different species, however, do sometimes mate and, if they are similar enough in species, can have offspring – for example, tigers and lions, buffalo and domestic cattle. But humans are not close enough to any other animal to have offspring.

27. *What is '69'?*

This is the slang name for the position in sexual play

where both male and female have oral-genital contact at the same time.

28. *What is sado-masochism?*

This is a contraction of two words, 'sadism', meaning to get sexual pleasure from giving pain to someone, and 'masochism', meaning to get sexual pleasure from pain inflicted by someone else. The words are combined because most people who get some sexual pleasure from hurting others also get it from being hurt. People often use these words in a non-sexual way, applying 'sadist' to people who seem to enjoy hurting other people and 'masochist' to those who appear to get satisfaction out of being humiliated. This, however, is really an incorrect usage.

There is a little sado-masochism in all of us. For example, people who are aroused sexually often enjoy nibbling, biting or scratching. A few people develop much stronger behaviour in this direction. They enjoy being beaten, whipped, tied down or similar situations. Boys and girls sometimes think of such activity when they masturbate or at other times. But there is no cause to worry unless these things are put into practice.

29. *What is incest?*

Legally, incest is having sexual intercourse with a relative of the opposite sex. This relative could be mother, father, brother, sister, grandparents or grandchildren. It also includes adopted children, though probably not, as the law now stands, step-children. In its broader sense, incest does not necessarily mean sexual intercourse, but includes any kind of sexual relations, even homosexual, between relatives. Sex play with sisters and cousins, however, is not at all unusual in pre-adolescence.

The incest taboo is the oldest of them all, going back to earliest times, and it is the strongest. Guilt alone makes a strong inhibition, and, of course, all religions absolutely forbid it. There are also medical reasons for the taboo. The children of an incestuous union will be likely to inherit the outstanding good characteristics of both. Genetically, however, continuing incestuous relationships in a group tend to 'breed out' – that is, the bad traits eventually overcome the good ones in successive generations.

30. *Should children be allowed to run around the house without any clothes on?*

It is one of the paradoxes of human life that we are told constantly and in many ways how beautiful the human body is, yet we are ashamed to show it in front of other people except within certain limits, of which the bikini is the extreme. This need to cover the body is as old as Adam, in one sense. Originally people covered themselves as protection from the weather, but in time it became a matter of religion, and in our own society it is a heritage from the strict religious feelings of Puritanism. Consequently people cannot be so free as some might like to be, short of joining a nudist colony, because they will feel the weight of society's displeasure. It is possible to be more relaxed about nudity in the privacy of the home – if, in that home, the standards are different from those in society at large. Parents still set these standards for the most part. To a large extent, they determine how much nudity is permitted, and where and when. No matter what is decreed, the human body remains beautiful and one need feel no shame in viewing it.

31. *What is a douche (pronounced doōsh)?*

In Chapter 8, I mentioned the douche as a means of washing out semen from the vagina in order not to become pregnant. Douching for this purpose is highly ineffective. Most doctors believe too frequent douching can be harmful, because it washes out natural lubricating liquids from the vagina. Unless there is some infection, most physicians advise against it. Washing with soap and water outside the sex organ to cleanse the secretions that form around the clitoris and inner lips particularly is sufficient.

32. *What is a miscarriage?*

A miscarriage (sometimes called a 'spontaneous abortion') is the loss of the foetus before it is able to live outside the mother. Some causes relate to the physical condition of the mother, like certain types of fibroid tumours (although a minority of them), tears in the womb mouth from childbirth or a misshapen uterus. Others result from general illnesses, like abnormal gland function, chronic high blood pressure, uncontrolled diabetes, untreated syphilis, severe undernourishment and high temperatures. Careful medical supervision can forestall miscarriage in diabetics and women with high blood pressure.

These physical causes are in the minority. Most miscarriages result from what is called by doctors 'defective germ plasm'. Almost three out of four human miscarriages are the result of defective eggs. A foetus which develops improperly usually dies and is expelled from the body as foreign material by muscular contractions of the uterus. A defective-germ-plasm conception usually stops developing after six or seven weeks, but is carried in the uterus for three or four weeks longer. Consequently a miscarriage occurs usually around the tenth or eleventh week of pregnancy.

Contrary to popular opinion, few miscarriages are caused by a blow or a jolt or an emotional upheaval. Most doctors agree, as one specialist puts it, that 'you cannot shake a good human egg loose, any more than fresh wind will cause healthy ripe apples to fall from the tree'.

Miscarriage usually offers virtually no risk to a woman, although she may bleed enough to require a transfusion, and she should recover in a few days.

33. *What is sodomy?*

The word comes from the biblical town of Sodom, the sinful city, in which people were supposed to be involved in 'unnatural sexual practices'. We have no idea what these practices really were. Sodomy has sometimes meant any homosexual practice, or putting the mouth on the sex organs of another person, whether in homosexual or heterosexual contact, or any anal intercourse whether homosexual or heterosexual, or any contact between humans and other animals.

34. *What does the expression 'female complaint' mean?*

It refers to any sort of physical complaint women have in connection with their sex organs. This would include trouble with menstruation, the vagina, the ovaries or the uterus.

35. *What does 'Caesarian birth' mean?*

It is the birth of a baby through the abdominal wall. The uterus is cut open and the baby is taken directly out of it without passing through the vagina. This is done if the baby is too large, or is in the wrong position, or if the mother has some physical condition which would make regular birth too difficult. In modern medical practice, it is not a dangerous operation and many women have perfectly healthy babies delivered by this method.

36. *Does a man ever urinate in a woman during intercourse?*

No. It is very difficult for a man to urinate with an erect penis, and it is difficult to have intercourse without an erection.

37. *What does a man do when he rapes a woman?*

'To rape' means 'to have intercourse by force'. Theoretically it is impossible to rape a woman, but there are all kinds of possible force. For example, if a man were to pin a woman down with his body and struggle with her for a long time until she no longer struggled, then had intercourse with her, that would be considered rape. Again, the use of intimidation, fraud or trickery to force a woman into complying would be rape. According to law, a girl under the age of sixteen, is technically unable to give consent. Any intercourse, even if the girl is willing, is called 'unlawful sexual intercourse', if she is under the prescribed age.

38. *What is a foetus?*

Any unborn baby. Up to seven weeks, this is also known as an 'embryo'.

39. *How does artificial insemination work?*

Sometimes the husband cannot make his wife pregnant, either because he hasn't manufactured enough sperm, or the sperm died before reaching the egg, or for several other reasons, some physical and some psychological. In these cases, it is sometimes possible to inject his semen into his wife artificially and she becomes pregnant. In other cases, it is necessary to use the semen of another man. This can be placed in the vagina by the doctor in his office. The women never see the donor. Consequently there are women who have babies without having their husband impregnate them. It is estimated that artificial insemination is used in one to two hundred cases a year in Great Britain.

40. *What is the difference in pubic hair between men and women?*

A woman's is finer and silkier, like the hair on her head. A woman's pubic hair is also distributed more in the shape of a triangle, wider at the top. Some boys think they can tell if the colour of a girl's hair is natural if it is the same colour as her pubic hair. Actually, the real comparison is with the eyebrows. A blonde girl's pubic hair will tend to be darker than her head hair, a brunette's will be lighter. As people get older, pubic hair tends to become grey, although at a much slower rate than head hair.

In boys, the hair grows around the penis, especially directly above it, and in some, as they grow older, a line of hair grows up to the navel. This is called the '*linea alba*'. A few girls also have this line. There is also some pubic hair that grows from a boy's scrotum, and even behind it, to and around the anus.

A girl's pubic hair does not interfere with intercourse because there is none on the inner lip of the vulva or even on the inside of the outer lips.

41. *How do hospitals tell if a girl has been raped?*

In reality, they can't tell. They can determine if she has had intercourse recently if there is still some semen in the vagina. Bruises or scratches, freshly inflicted, may indicate the use of force. If a girl's hymen has been broken by the act, it may still be bleeding, or there will be traces of it, and this is another piece of evidence. But as we have seen in question 37, it would be difficult to determine, in a physical sense, whether rape has occurred or not.

42. *Suppose a girl has intercourse and menstruates some time afterwards. Is she pregnant?*

A few girls menstruate a time or two after they become pregnant, but in the great majority it stops when pregnancy begins.

43. *What is menopause?*

Menopause, or 'change of life', or 'the change', should be understood by girls (and by boys, too) because their mothers will be experiencing it. Between forty-five and fifty-five, usually, women stop producing an egg cell every month. This is not a serious loss at that age, especially since menstruation will also cease. However, the female hormone (oestrogen) may also somewhat diminish and this may produce uncomfortable feelings. Doctors have learned how to treat this normal stage of a woman's life with additional hormones. In any case, her sexual life will not change but will go on exactly as it was before menopause.

MORE ABOUT PENGUINS
AND PELICANS

Penguinews, which appears every month, contains details of all the new books issued by Penguins as they are published. From time to time it is supplemented by *Penguins in Print*, which is a complete list of all books published by Penguins which are in print. (There are well over three thousand of these.)

A specimen copy of *Penguinews* will be sent to you free on request, and you can become a subscriber for the price of the postage. For a year's issues (including the complete lists) please send 30p if you live in the United Kingdom, or 60p if you live elsewhere. Just write to Dept EP, Penguin Books Ltd, Harmondsworth, Middlesex, enclosing a cheque or postal order, and your name will be added to the mailing list.

Some other books published by Penguins are described on the following pages.

Note : *Penguinews* and *Penguins in Print* are not available in the U.S.A. or Canada

BOYS AND SEX

Wardell B. Pomeroy

In this companion book, Dr Pomeroy, co-author of the two Kinsey reports, advises and informs adolescent boys, from an impartial and unbiased standpoint, about their natural sex-drives.

Dealing in a clear and honest manner with all aspects of sexual development, from masturbation and homosexuality to petting and intercourse, and with an enlightening 'question and answer' section, this book will guide boys towards a guilt-free understanding of the emotions and reactions which they will experience throughout adolescence.

At no time does Dr Pomeroy pose as the stern moralist: his aim is to overcome the guilt and anxiety which he feels are the enemies of a healthy sex life, and, as he states, to 'convey to children a sense of self-respect, responsibility, openness and the pleasurableness of sex'.

NOT FOR SALE IN THE U.S.A. OR CANADA

THE PSYCHOLOGY OF CHILDHOOD
AND ADOLESCENCE

C. I. Sandström

In this concise study of the processes of growing up Professor Sandström has produced a book which, although it is perfectly suited to the initial needs of university students and teachers in training, will appeal almost as much to parents and ordinary readers. His text covers the whole story of human physical and mental growth from conception to puberty.

Outlining the scope and history of developmental psychology, Professor Sandström goes on to detail the stages of growth in the womb, during the months after birth, and (year by year) up to the age of ten. There follow chapters on physical development, learning and perception, motivation, language and thought, intelligence, the emotions, social adjustment, and personality. The special conditions of puberty and of schooling are handled in the final chapters.

Throughout this masterly study the author necessarily refers to 'norms of development': these neatly represent the average stages of growing up, but (as Professor Mace comments in his introduction) they must only be applied to individual children with caution.

THE SEXUAL BEHAVIOUR OF
YOUNG PEOPLE

Michael Schofield

This report sets out to supply facts in an area in which sensation has tended to flourish. Michael Schofield's findings are based on the results of some 2,000 interviews held in England with young people between the ages of thirteen and nineteen.

The first fact to emerge is that sexual promiscuity, though it certainly exists, is not a prominent feature of teenage behaviour. Consequently the risk of venereal disease among the young is not high: infections, it is true, have increased lately, but less in this age-group than in others. Illegitimacy, according to this report, presents a graver problem: of every three girls who have premarital sexual intercourse, one can expect to become pregnant.

Scare reports about immorality and disease have raised a cry for improved sex education. Statistics given in this book certainly suggest that the majority of adolescents still receive little or no guidance from parents or teachers. The facts of contraception and venereal disease are almost outside their ken.

Michael Schofield's meticulous and balanced survey provides the kind of evidence (and the stimulus) needed for framing a sound plan of education and advice about sex for the young.

NOT FOR SALE IN THE U.S.A.

Also available
The Strange Case of Pot

CAREERS FOR GIRLS

Ruth Miller

Second Edition – revised and enlarged

Whether you are practical or artistic, better with people or with facts and figures, happier in an office, a laboratory or out of doors, *Careers for Girls* offers you a mass of information about jobs in well over a hundred different fields.

'There is a short description of the work involved, prospects, training, pay, personal attributes, further information, grants and, finally, related careers. Great care has been taken to make this information accurate, yet readable by the average girl in search of ideas' – *The Times Educational Supplement*.

'An admirable new reference book which should be in every school library' – *Daily Mirror*.

'Answers every question any sixth-former might want to know about qualifications, training, prospects and how to go about getting a job' – Mary Rand in the *Sunday Mirror*.

'Practical, imaginative and invaluable' – *Observer*.